The West of Wild Bill Hickok

THE WEST OF WILD BILL HICKOK

OF

WILD BILL HICKOK

Joseph G. Rosa

University of Oklahoma Press:Norman

By Joseph G. Rosa

The West of Wild Bill Hickok (Norman, 1982)
They Called Him Wild Bill: The Life and Adventures of James Butler Hickok (Norman, 1964; second edition, 1974)
Alias Jack McCall (Kansas City, 1967)
The Gunfighter: Man or Myth? (Norman, 1969)
Colonel Colt, London (London, 1976)

With Robin May

The Pleasure of Guns (London, 1974)
Gunsmoke: A Study of Violence in the Wild West (London, 1977)
Cowboy: The Man and the Myth (London, 1980)

Library of Congress Cataloging in Publication Data

Rosa, Joseph G.
  The West of Wild Bill Hickok.

  Bibliography: p. 209
  Includes index.
  1. Hickok, Wild Bill, 1837-1876—Iconography.   2. Peace officers—West (U.S.)—Iconography.   3. Scouts and scouting—West (U.S.)—Iconography.   I. Title.
F594.H62R67   978'.02'0924 [B]   81-21945
                                              AACR2

To Ethel Hickok

without whose help and understanding
this pictorial biography of her
Uncle James could not
have been written

Contents

Chapter Three: Plainsman   70

Plates

Chapter Four: Peace Officer and Pistoleer   102

Plates

Chapter Five: Showman   140

Plates

Plates

Preface

The purpose of this book is to reproduce in one volume all the known portraits of Wild Bill Hickok, together with a selection of photographs of his family, his friends, his foes, and the places that knew him. It was inspired by comments from reviewers of the second edition of *They Called Him Wild Bill* (University of Oklahoma Press, 1974), particularly one by Gary L. Roberts. Writing in *Nebraska History* (Spring, 1976), he lamented the fact that, although I had included some rare and interesting photographs of Wild Bill, I had also discarded all but one of those that had appeared in the first edition. "By eliminating these photographs," he declared, "the editors at Oklahoma missed an opportunity to present a photographic essay of exceptional merit."

Whether the inclusion of all the photographs would really have produced such a volume is debatable, for the publisher's first consideration had been one of space in what was already a lengthy text. But having made his point, the reviewer left me the task of deciding how such a presentation should be made. The simple answer was a short book. I realized, of course, that there would be problems, because little was known about when and where photographs of Hickok were made, and by whom. This led to a lot of research, and, although some questions remain unanswered, much new information has come to light.

It is worth remembering that Hickok's lifetime (1837-76) spanned the very period that gave birth to photography and witnessed many of its improvements. He was barely two years old when, with the introduction of the daguerreotype—the process perfected by the Frenchman Louis Daguerre—photography first became appreciated in the United States. To produce daguerreotypes, highly polished, silvered surfaces of copper plates were sensitized in the camera and developed with mercury vapor.

In the early 1840s the Englishman William Henry Fox Talbot produced sensitized paper negatives—calotypes—but they did not meet with the success of the daguerreotypes. In 1851 both processes were rivaled by the ambrotypes. These were reproductions on glass. The plate was sensitized in a bath of silver nitrate and exposed while it was still wet. A positive image was obtained by placing dark paper or cloth behind the exposed plate, or by coating it with varnish or paint. If the backing was impermanent, the plates could be used as negatives for making paper prints.

A cheaper and enormously more popular process, which competed with the daguerreotypes and ambrotypes, produced ferrotypes (sometimes called melainotypes). These were commonly called "tintypes" because they were produced on sheet iron; like daguerreotypes, they gave a reverse or mirror image.

Soon afterward, in 1858-59, came the more familiar photographs printed on paper. These were called *cartes de visites*, or "pictorial visiting cards." Small paper prints gummed either to plain cards or to cards imprinted with the photographer's or retailer's name, they sold in the millions. They, too, were later replaced by larger prints called cabinet photographs, and, in the years following Hickok's death, further refinements culminated in modern gelatin dry-plate photography and halftone prints for illustrating periodicals and books.

During the course of my research for this book I found twenty-four photographs purported to be of Wild Bill, but several more may yet come to light. When examining these photographs, I readily appreciated why doubt has been cast upon some of them, for appearances can be deceptive. In their recollections contemporaries and family members claim that Hickok was light-skinned, his face freckled, his eyes blue-gray, his hair and eyebrows an auburn or tawny hue, and his mustache straw-colored. It is regrettable that some retouchers either ignored or were unaware of these details, and their efforts are little more than mutilations. To further complicate matters, the chemicals used in Hickok's day were not as sensitive to color and tone as those employed in modern panchromatic films, and his hair, whether dry or greased in the manner of the plainsmen, looks darker than it really was; in some photographs it appears to be black. In reproducing his photographs I have therefore tried to include only the best prints available; where necessary, mutilations are included for comparison.

Several woodcuts based upon photographs also appear, and their presence will be explained hereafter. I have kept the text strictly chronological and linked to the main captions. Some material is new and was discovered too late for inclusion in the 1974 edition of the biography. Its inclusion or mention here is essential to the narrative.

In presenting this small volume of photographs devoted to Wild Bill and his West, I hope that the reader will appreciate not only the subject but also the tremendous debt we owe to those courageous, and frequently nameless, old-time photographers, who, despite hardship and danger, crossed and re-crossed the American West to preserve for this and future generations a graphic record of a people and a time long gone but far from forgotten.

Joseph G. Rosa
Ruislip, Middlesex, England

Acknowledgments

My dedication acknowledges the great debt I owe to Ethel Hickok, but there is also one other member of the family to whom I extend my sincere thanks. She is Edith Andrews Harmon, the family historian, whose assistance and encouragement, together with the donation of an original photograph purported to be of Wild Bill, is greatly appreciated.

Special thanks must also be extended to Nyle H. Miller and Joseph W. Snell, who, in their capacities as officers of the Kansas State Historical Society, and as personal friends of many years standing, have allowed me access to many of the photographs reproduced in this volume. The staff of that society also deserves a special thanks for the great courtesy they have always shown me, even when some of my requests were quite obscure.

I have also enjoyed a mutual exchange of information and photographs with Alys Freeze, former head of the Western History Department, and James Davis, formerly of the Photographic Section, Denver Public Library; Jack D. Haley and Emily Myers of the Western History Collections, University of Oklahoma, who unraveled many mysteries; and Reed Whitaker, chief, and Bob Knecht, of the Archives Branch, Federal Archives and Record Center, Kansas City, Missouri. Similarly, it has been my pleasure since the 1950s to work with the state historical societies or libraries of Colorado, Connecticut, Illinois, Nebraska, New York, South Dakota, and Wyoming.

Others to whom I owe a debt for information, for photographs, and for great assistance are listed alphabetically as follows: Frank Aydelotte; F. C. Bannon; William Bell; Fred Borsch; Carmen Bria, Jr.; Emory Canty, Jr.; Arthur Carmody; R. C. Corbyn; Colin Crocker; Jack DeMattos; the late Mary Everhard; Mrs. Jean Fisherkeller; the late Earl R. Forrest; John S. Gray; the late Horace A. Hickok; the late Howard L. Hickok and his son James Butler Hickok; Ida Ipe; Mrs. Sue Herzog-Johnson; Paul King; Cliff and Doris Leonard;

Jo Lohoefener; Robert E. McNellis; Richard Marohn, M.D.; Watson Parker; Chuck Parsons; Herb Peck, Jr.; David R. Phillips; Roy and Joyce Piper; the late Paul D. Riley; Gary L. Roberts; Martha A. Sandweiss, curator of photographs, the Amon Carter Museum of Western Art, Fort Worth, Texas; William B. Secrest; Robert M. Utley; the late Stewart P. Verckler; Durrett Wagner; John Wickman; and Larry Wilson. And a special thanks to Paul and Penny Dalton who processed many of the photographs used in this book.

To all these people and organizations, and to any I may have inadvertently neglected to mention, my grateful thanks.

Photographs not otherwise acknowledged are from my own collection.

J. G. R.

The West of Wild Bill Hickok

Fig. 1. *Wild Bill as depicted in* Harper's New Monthly Magazine. *See Plate 44.*

Introduction

Wild Bill Hickok proved on many occasions that he was not gun-shy, and, as evidenced by the number of his photographs that have survived, neither was he afraid of the camera. Yet it seems that few of his contemporaries were aware of these photographs. For some, his features remained a memory undimmed by time, but for others, old age had played them false, and genuine photographs of Hickok went unrecognized, or else their authenticity was challenged.

One reason for their confusion may be that until the early years of this century the only published portraits of Wild Bill were woodcuts or steel engravings. The first of these appeared in the February, 1867, issue of *Harper's New Monthly Magazine*, and is reproduced as Figure 1. Although a good likeness, it did not have the accuracy of the photograph from which it was made; nor did the 1872 woodcut (Figure 2), also from a photograph, that was published in W. E. Webb's *Buffalo Land*. Unlike the *Harper's* illustration, however, Webb's original photograph is available for comparison.

Similarly, woodcuts of Wild Bill published in William F. Cody's 1879 autobiography[1] and J. W. Buel's work[2] were both made from photographs, and, as can be seen from Figures 3 and 4, they were good likenesses. It was not until the end of the nineteenth century, however, that actual photographs of Wild Bill were published in books, newspapers, and magazines.

Few original photographs of Hickok have survived, and only two glass plates are known. Apart from two tintypes in his family's possession, most of those I know are *cartes de visites*. Unfortunately, few of these photographs are correctly credited, for photographers customarily copied or retailed the work of others, and it is often they who are credited today. Only time may prove just who was responsible for some of the disputed photographs.

Such detail meant little to the old-timers who had known Hickok, however. They were only too delighted to be shown photographs of him. Some

Fig. 2. *A woodcut from a photograph reproduced in W. E. Webb's* Buffalo Land. *See Plate 73b.*

Fig. 3 *(page 5, left). A woodcut from a photograph credited to Rockwood and reproduced in Cody's* Life of the Honorable William Frederick Cody. *See Plate 101a.*

Fig. 4 *(page 5, right). A woodcut made from a photograph credited to D. D. Dare. See Plate 106a.*

of them had never seen any, but to others, like Timothy P. Hersey, the photographs brought back a flood of memories. Hersey was the first settler in what became Abilene, Kansas. In a letter to J. B. Edwards, written from Castle Rock, Washington, on January 5, 1905, he said: "I am glad to see his visage once more. We were raised close together in Ills. I knew him when he was 12 years old."[3]

Another grateful recipient of a photograph was Charles F. Gross, who had worked as a bookkeeper for Joseph G. McCoy in Abilene. He informed Edwards: "I have no picture[s] of Wild Bill. I did have but they have been stolen from me[.] If you have an extra send me one please."[4]

J. B. Edwards was an early resident of Abilene and, by his own account, was once arrested by Hickok for discharging a firearm within city limits. He lived to the ripe old age of 106. Edwards apparently was quite generous with prints, and few of them were refused. The photograph in question was one that he claimed Hickok had given to him. The Topeka *State Journal* of February 20, 1937, published this version of how he acquired it:

> *Wild Bill, during his stay in Abilene, traveled over to Junction City where he had Photographer A. P. Trott make his picture.*
> *On the day of his departure [from town following his term as City*

WILD BILL.

Marshal] he came into the bank to present a copy of the photograph to the president. Edwards was in the bank at that time.

"I was standing there, he saw me and gave me one, too."

Edwards is proud of that picture of Wild Bill Hickok. The original was copied [recopied?] recently and Edwards sent Cecil B. DeMille one of the copies to assist the director in the making of "The Plainsman" film.

Edwards's photograph is believed to be that reproduced as Plate 91a. He rediscovered it in 1899 and had it copied by Forney of Abilene, who in turn sold many cabinet-sized prints mounted on thick cards. The original Trott photograph owned by Edwards has disappeared, but the one used in this book is a copy from a very old print that Edwards donated to the Dickinson County Historical Society in Abilene. Some years ago I was able to examine a *carte de visite* of this photograph that bore A. P. Trott's imprint.

Trott has long been credited with making one or perhaps more plates of Wild Bill, but copies are scarce, and even less familiar than his work is the life story of this early-day photographer. It has been established that he arrived in Junction City, Kansas, early in 1868. The Junction City *Weekly Union* reported on April 4, 1868, that

few, if any, places west of St. Louis, can boast of as fine [a] picture gallery as Junction and one of a better artist. Mr. A. P. Trott, besides

5

being an urbane and thorough gentleman, understands his profession perfectly. He has but recently established himself in our city, and already his business is rapidly increasing. . . . His gallery is on the corner of Washington and 8th streets.

During this time Trott's young wife died, and thereafter he worked with special diligence at his business, which continued to expand. Within a year he was described as the taker of ambrotypes, ferrotypes, melainotypes, and tintypes, and as having perfected a means of producing pictures on pearly surfaces, cottonwood shingle, and porcelain. By 1871 he had become a regular advertiser in the Abilene *Chronicle,* and occasionally his advertisements in that and other newspapers called upon his customers to "secure the shadow 'ere the substance fades."[5]

Another of Edwards's many correspondents who expressed an interest in Hickok photographs was George W. Hansen. He was the man whose earnest research unearthed the original court records of the incident at Rock Creek, Nebraska Territory, on July 12, 1861, when Hickok was involved in the killing of David C. McCanles and two other men. Aware that some dubious photographs were even then in circulation, he remarked:

> *Another matter is that of the photographs of Hickok. I was sure, after my conversation with you, that you had a genuine photograph of him, taken in his prime, just when he would be in the handsomest period of his life; and without any disparagement to his appearance, nobody would say that he was the "handsomest man in America," as he is described by Connelley. Your reference to faked photographs of Hickok also explains why Connelley's photograph of Hickok [reproduced as the frontispiece in Vol. XVII of the Kansas State Historical Society's* Collections *(1926-28)] looks no more like yours than it does like you or me. He surely had a copy of your genuine photo in his possession, but it was not pretty enough for his purpose. I notice that your photo of Hickok closely resembles the picture used by Nichols in the Harper's Magazine story. . . . I have sometimes thought I would write an article "On the Portraits of Wild Bill."*
>
> *I have had photograph copies taken of a pen sketch made of Hickok the week he was shot. It is interesting to compare it with your genuine photograph of him. I have only newspaper pictures taken from your photo, but they are fair copies— one from K. C. Star, and one from Burns in Ford's Independent.*[6]

Fig. 5. *Wild Bill, from a sketch discovered in 1918.*

No trace of the pen-and-ink sketch mentioned by Hansen has come to light; but perhaps it was the one brought to my attention some years ago by the late Vincent Mercaldo. It was originally a pencil drawing that turned up in a junk shop in New York in 1918. Mercaldo wrote: "The drawing of Wild Bill Hickok was just a head with his hat on showing part of his bust. The original was done on pulp newspaper while he was playing cards, and this fell apart. But not before I made a careful copy in Indian ink. . . . this was back in 1925."[7] Mercaldo then kindly sketched it on his letter, and the pen-and-ink drawing reproduced as Figure 5 is a faithful copy of it.

In 1933 the late Herbert Cody Blake, an eccentric man who made many claims and counterclaims about various Westerners, corresponded with the late Robert Taft who was then engaged in extensive photographic research. On June 15, Blake informed Taft that he had not only "2700 negatives of Old Western folks, places & events," but also "the best & largest collection of photos of J. B. Hickok, Wild Bill & Calamity Jane Known." On July 3 he promised that he would mail "a bunch of Wild Bills—Copy any you care for." When I went through the Taft Collection, I found only one photograph of Hickok. This was a slide of the alleged Trott portrait.

Evidently, Taft in his turn asked Blake about alleged Hickok signatures and whether he ever signed any of his photographs. This prompted the reply: "As for autograph[s], he certainly never aut[ographed] one 'Wild Bill.' I never knew of his *ever* auto[graphing] a photo—Objecting to it he was never called

7

Wild Bill to his face. I'm told this by 3 of his old pals—and of the doz[en] pistols m[ar]k[e]d "JBH"—"Wild Bill" etc[.,] all are fakes."[8]

Despite such assurance, photographs of Wild Bill bearing his alleged signature are known; their authenticity will be dealt with elsewhere. As for his dislike of "Wild Bill," this is nonsense. Letters from him to various newspapers and at least two letters that he wrote to his wife bear his real name and his alias.

As we have seen, interest in photographs of Wild Bill is not by any means confined to modern researchers. Indeed, at least one eminent individual of Hickok's time professed to own plates. William A. Bell, a former chief photographer for the Army Medical Museum at Washington, D.C. (and no relation to the William A. Bell who wrote *New Tracks in North America*), was active both in the Mexican War and the Civil War. He later joined several government expeditions before establishing himself in Philadelphia, where his portraits and experiments with dry-plate photography were widely acclaimed. Writing from Sigourney, Iowa, on October 19, 1905, he offered Frank A. Root, coauthor of *The Overland Stage to California*, the opportunity of exchanging prints of Root's portraits of Jim Bridger, Kit Carson, and California Joe for copies of his own portraits of Hickok:

> *I have some of the orig[in]al negatives of Wild Bill, and [I am] going to have some photos taken from the same, and as you are one of the Old Boys, of the Plains, if you would like to have a photograph I shall send you one with pleasure, as soon as I have got them finished. I have had the neg[a]tive sent to a photo establishment in Ottunwa, so as to have the best photos made from it that I can get. I have carried the negative, all over the country with me, and it got some scratched, it was taken in Abilene[,] Kansas at [the] time Wild Bill was Marshall [sic], they are small photo[s] about 3 x 4 inches, but they are nice ones.[9]*

William Bell died in his eightieth year on January 28, 1910, and efforts to track down his photographs and alleged plates of Hickok have so far proved fruitless.[10]

In more recent years the search for photographs of Hickok and other Western characters has become widespread, and several interesting portraits have come to light. Vincent Mercaldo, who started his archive soon after World War I, built an impressive collection of original photographs. He and I corresponded for a number of years, and shortly before his death we exchanged prints of Wild Bill. It was Mercaldo's belief that George Rockwood

made three of the best-known Hickok portraits and that others, among them
Jeremiah Gurney, simply copied them and sold them as their own.

He substantiated this claim by producing a cabinet-size full-face portrait
of Hickok, mounted on a card bearing Rockwood's imprint, and the original
glass plate of the left-side-face portrait, which he assured me was also by
Rockwood. The third portrait, a right-side-face view, was, however, credited
to Sarony, 680 Broadway, and it is this photograph (reproduced as Plate
101*b*) that has been found with Gurney's and other photographers' imprints.
The original *carte de visite* in my collection is credited to the Majilton Photographing Company of Philadelphia.

After Mercaldo's death I found what is perhaps the rarest of Hickok's
portraits (Plate 98*a*). It is credited to Gurney & Son, which suggests that
Hickok was photographed by several New York photographers or that they
copied each other's work indiscriminately. It should be stressed, however, that
both Gurney and Rockwood were well-respected rivals. Jeremiah Gurney
began his career as a daguerreotypist in the 1840s and is believed to have
died about 1890, by which time the firm had been known as Gurney & Son
for some years. His last listing in the New York City directories was in 1890.
His son Benjamin continued the business, and his address was listed as 37
Union Square. George Rockwood, however, was not established in New York
until 1859. In the early 1870s he was listed at 17 Union Square, but by 1909
the company had several addresses, and from 1911 it was listed in the name
of George Rockwood, Jr., his father presumably having died the year before.[11]

In describing how he acquired such a prize as an original glass plate
credited to Rockwood, Mercaldo wrote:

> *The late Albert Davis was my very close friend for the last eight years of
> his life, [and] during our friendship the old fellow and myself became
> very close. All the best photos in my collection came from him one by
> one. I have the Albert Davis negative, plus his photo of Hickok, also
> [the group photograph of] Hickok, Texas Jack and Cody was given to me,
> and many others. . . . He died about 26 years ago. Now I'm the old-man
> of the picture collections.*
>
> *The glass plate of Hickok was among the H[erbert] Cody Blake stuff
> and was in very poor shape, and the emulsion on all 4 sides started to
> fall off, [and] all that remains [now] is his face and some of the bust.
> This I managed to save and it is in good shape.[12]*

In discussing the photograph of Hickok staring straight at the camera, which has appeared in many versions, some of them very poor, Mercaldo wrote: "White and Grabill made copies of this . . . and claimed them as their own. They were poor copies at that, and it was their prints that went around being re-copied over and over."[13]

I have examined some of the copies sold by White, and I agree that the retouching is bad. Surprisingly, Buffalo Bill Cody accepted them without question and made a practice of presenting copies to his friends. Ethel Hickok, Wild Bill's niece, has a large framed portrait credited to White that was given to her father by Cody at the turn of the century.

In 1960 I learned that Mary E. Everhard, of Leavenworth, Kansas, owned an original photograph of Wild Bill that she dated at 1855. For a modest sum she sold me a copy, but I was disappointed to find that it had been heavily retouched. I explained to her why I thought it was made about 1867 rather than 1855 and then asked her if I might have an unretouched print from the original plate for publication. She was at first reluctant to provide a print from the original plate because, as a skilled photographer and retoucher, it was her policy never to let clients see unretouched portraits of themselves, and prints of Wild Bill were not to be exempt. Thanks to some prompting from her lawyer, however, she finally agreed, and I received the print. It proved to be a remarkable portrait, and she assured me that neither of these versions had ever been published.[14]

It turned out that she was mistaken, however, because when I was examining a scrapbook in the Connelley Collection at the Denver Public Library in 1972, I found a newspaper reproduction of the photograph that had been published in the 1920s (possibly in a Sunday supplement), but the newspaper was not dated or credited to any particular publication. Unlike the two bust photographs that Miss Everhard had provided, this version was three-quarter length and showed Hickok's waistcoat and shirt front partly unbottoned. A watch chain hung down to a fob pocket, and around his waist was what appeared to be a dark sash or belt. Sadly, Miss Everhard had died before my discovery, but the original plate exists, and in 1977 I was allowed to examine it.

The plate was made about 1867 or 1868 by Ebenezer Elijah Henry, an Englishman who practiced in Canada before his arrival in the United States. He reached Leavenworth in 1864 and remained there until his death in 1917 at the age of ninety. The business was then taken over by his stepson, Harrison Putney. When Putney died in 1950 at the age of eighty-six, Miss Everhard carried on, and not long before her own death in 1970 she sold the Hickok plate and the rest of her collection of over forty thousand glass and celluloid plates to David R. Phillips, of Chicago, who published a number of the original Henry plates in book form. Phillips has since sold the Hickok plate and a number of other Leavenworth items to the Amon Carter Museum at Fort Worth, Texas. Before the sale, Phillips very kindly allowed me to examine the original plate and several prints, and the freckles and other facial blemishes on Hickok's features are very clear.[15]

Hickok's face has also attracted the attention of artists and others eager to read more into his features than is apparent in photographs. An interesting statement was made by one DeLester Sackett, described as a pioneer Western photographer and later a lecturer on phrenology. He expressed the following opinion concerning Hickok:

> *The student of physiognomy will find an interesting study in the lines of this man's face. Temperamentally the motive of bone and muscular system predominates, as indicated by the oblong square-shape of the face. The remarkable thing about this face, however, is the absence of curved lines. It is made up of straight lines and sharp angles.*
>
> *Note the straight line of the eyebrows, the straight line from the top of the ear to the angle of the jaw, then to the corner of the chin, the square chin itself, the straight line of the mouth, the straight line from the end of the nose back to the wings of the nostrils, the straight line of the upper lobe of the ears, which stands at right angles to the lines of forehead over the ears. And finally note how the hair grows, a straight line at the top of the forehead, at right angles with the lines on each side. The whole face shows resolution, courage and determination, in a marked degree. The expression of the face is one of sadness and kindness.*
>
> *I knew this man, the bravest man I ever met. His physiognomy was a true index to his character.*[16]

Despite Sackett's conclusion, it must be remembered that when one looks for "character" in Hickok's or any other Western figure's features, the facial expression is rarely natural. This, of course, is the result of the time required for exposure, during which the sitter had to endure sometimes ill-fitting neck clamps. The exposures varied. In the early days of photography it meant minutes, but later the time was reduced to seconds. Nonetheless, the result still produced a wooden appearance.

Researching Hickok the man was a fascinating exercise, and attempting to identify and place his photographs has been an experience in itself. Perhaps I, too, in some small measure, have succeeded, in Trott's words, in "securing the shadow" now that the "substance has faded."

CHAPTER ONE

The Beckoning West
(1837-1861)

James Butler Hickok came from Illinois. Although it was no longer a wilderness, it was nonetheless still a part of the frontier when he was born on May 27, 1837, at Homer (later renamed Troy Grove), a village in the northern part of the state.[1] Memories of the bloody Black Hawk War five years earlier still hindered settlement, despite the removal of the Indians west of the Mississippi River, where they were under the protection and supervision of the United States government. By 1850, however, Illinois was regarded as settled, and by the mid-1850s it boasted a large farming community.

The opening up of the Kansas Territory for settlement in 1854 prompted the Hickoks to consider taking up farming land there, but the slavery issue was an impediment to them. Like the Hickoks, most Kansans were antislavery, whereas proslavery Missourians, fearful that the territory would become a haven for escaped slaves, were determined that Kansas should become a slave state. Hundreds of persons crossed the border and laid claim to land, and so began the struggle between the Kansas "Free Staters" and the Missouri "Border Ruffians."[2]

Despite such dangers, James and his brother Lorenzo set off for Kansas in June, 1856, to see for themselves what opportunities there were, but, upon learning that their mother was ill, Lorenzo returned home, leaving James to carry on alone. James sided with the Free Staters, and during the next four years he took part in the fighting in Kansas, became village constable of Monticello Township, Johnson County, and fell in love with the daughter of John Owen, an early settler in the area. But his family interfered when it learned that the girl was part Indian, and shortly afterwards James left Johnson

County. By late 1859, he was in the employ of Russell, Majors and Waddell as a teamster on the Santa Fe Trail.[3]

It was during this period that Hickok first met William Frederick Cody, immortalized as "Buffalo Bill." James became a welcome guest at the Cody home in Leavenworth and, according to his own family's recollections, paid only infrequent visits to Troy Grove, one of the earliest in 1859, but he was soon back on the plains.[4]

Early in 1861, Hickok was involved in an incident that is known to history as the "McCanles Massacre." First publicized in an article in the February, 1867, issue of *Harper's New Monthly Magazine*, it has since become a part of frontier legend.

According to *Harper's*, Hickok was guiding a detachment of cavalry from Camp Floyd to an undisclosed destination when he obtained permission to visit a friend of his, a Mrs. Waltman. Armed with only one revolver, he took a potshot at some turkeys along the way and killed one, meaning to have it for supper. At the cabin Mrs. Waltman greeted him with a scream: "Is that you, Bill? Oh, God! They will kill you! Run! run! They will kill you." The writer, Colonel George Ward Nichols, went on to tell a bloodcurdling tale: how Hickok was attacked by ten armed men and, despite some terrible wounds, somehow managed to shoot, stab, or bludgeon them all to death before he himself collapsed from exhaustion and loss of blood.[5]

It was a good story, and Nichols has received credit for first publicizing it in a national magazine, but the tale was already well known in parts of Kansas, Missouri, and Nebraska and was rapidly being assimilated into local folklore.[6] In reality, of course, no "massacre" occurred, and only three men were killed; historians still argue over the conflicting evidence. Although Nichols portrayed David C. McCanles, the principal character in the drama, as the leader of a gang of cutthroats, there was no such gang. McCanles, in the opinion of many of his neighbors, was merely a local bully and a "border ruffian." When Russell, Majors and Waddell had organized their Pony Express and made the first run on April 3, 1860, they also set up relay stations, one of them at Rock Creek, Nebraska Territory, on property that belonged to McCanles's "East-side ranch." At first they agreed to rent the property but later decided to buy it. Following negotiations with McCanles and a down payment of one third the price—the remainder to be paid in installments spread over three months—the company took possession of the station.[7]

Hickok arrived at Rock Creek early in March, 1861. He had been sent there by the company to act as a stock tender following an injury that is still shrouded in mystery (some claimed that it was the result of a bear fight). Whatever the cause, he was apparently unfit for normal duties and suffered a little from McCanles's rough sense of humor.

Russell, Majors and Waddell also dispatched a man named Horace Wellman to serve as station superintendent and with him was his common-law wife. The pair arrived at the East-side ranch in Rock Creek early in May. By late June the company's payments were in arrears, and McCanles persuaded Wellman to go to Benjamin Ficklin, the company's line superintendent at Brownville, to find out what was wrong. With Wellman he sent his twelve-year-old son, William Monroe McCanles, to obtain supplies and, while they were there, to see if he could recognize any of his father's stock and harness in the possession of the Rocky Mountain Dispatch Company, which had left Rock Creek owing him money.[8]

Wellman soon learned that the company was in financial difficulties and that Russell was in Washington for discussions with the government. On July 11 the pair returned to Rock Creek and made their report. Wellman learned that during his absence McCanles had made repeated demands upon those left at the station (including Hickok) to move out and let him take over the property. He also had accused Mrs. Wellman's father, who lived nearby, of stealing a horse and wagon from him and promptly beat him up.

On the afternoon of July 12, McCanles appeared at the East-side ranch accompanied by his son and two employees (his cousin James Woods and James Gordon). McCanles demanded his money or the return of his property. Wellman told him that he had no power to do either, but he wilted before McCanles and retreated to the house. Mrs. Wellman then started abusing McCanles and, moments later, was joined by Hickok, who stood in the doorway of the cabin. McCanles warned Hickok to keep out of the way, for the argument was none of his business. Hickok is alleged to have replied: "Perhaps 'tis or 'taint."[9]

Some have claimed that McCanles was armed with a shotgun and others that he was unarmed. To ease the tension or perhaps assess the situation, he asked for a drink of water. Hickok nodded and stepped back inside to get it, leaving McCanles standing outside the door. Moments later a shot was fired from within. As McCanles fell dying, his son rushed to him but was chased away by Mrs. Wellman. At the sound of the shot Woods and Gordon had run to the house from the barn, and Hickok shot them both. As Woods fell, Mrs. Wellman killed him with a grubbing hoe. Gordon, however, managed to escape into the brush, where he was found soon afterward and shot by one of the men from the station. Hickok, Wellman, and a Pony Express rider named J. W. ("Doc") Brink were arrested on July 15 on warrants sworn out by the McCanles family and were taken to Beatrice, Nebraska Territory. At a preliminary hearing the trio pleaded self-defense in the protection of company property and were released.[10]

Hickok's actual involvement in the affair is still unclear. Some insist that the McCanles party was unarmed and that Hickok and company shot them down in cold blood. Others believe that Wellman shot McCanles and that, while Hickok wounded Woods and Gordon, others in the party actually killed them. Curiously, when Charles Dawson published the first factual account of the incident in 1912, Monroe McCanles accepted his version; by the middle 1920s, however, he had changed his story yet again.[11] And there the case rests. Whatever the real truth of Rock Creek, it was, insofar as Hickok was concerned, the prelude to fame.

HICCOX

FOVET · ET · ORNAT

1a, b. *The Hickok family claim as a forebear one Edward Hiccox, Esq., of Stratford-upon-Avon, Warwickshire, England. Hiccox, Hiccocks, Hitchcock, and other variants of the name were common, and a family of that name were tenants of William Shakespeare. Research at the College of Arms in London has revealed that the Hiccox arms (Plate 1a) were never officially registered, unlike those of John Hiccocks (1b), who entered the Middle Temple in 1683, was admitted to the Bar in 1690, and was called to the Bench in 1709. A master of the High Court of Chancery from 1703 until 1723, he died in 1726. No direct link has been found between Edward Hiccox and John Hiccocks, but similarities in their arms suggest that one exists.*

The Hickok family was established in America by William Hickocks (sometimes spelled Hitchcock) in 1635. By the Revolutionary War period the Hickoks had spread over New England, and Aaron Hickok, Wild Bill's great-grandfather, either fought in or witnessed the Battle of Bunker Hill. He and his son Otis later fought in the War of 1812. Otis died from wounds received during the Battle of Sackets Harbor, and Aaron died the following year, having married twice and sired nineteen children. (W. J. G. Verco, C.V.O., Chester herald of arms, College of Arms, London, to the author, Nov. 5, 1970; Records of the Middle Temple Library, London; Edith Andrews Harmon, Another Man Named Hickok, *32, 44.)*

16

2. *The birthplace of Wild Bill Hickok has been a tourist attraction for decades, and the state of Illinois has long appreciated and acknowledged its debt to him. In 1929, ten thousand dollars was raised to provide a permanent memorial, and this rugged and unhewed mass of granite was the result. The bronze tablet inscription, believed to be the work of William E. Connelley, reads:*

JAMES BUTLER "WILD BILL" HICKOK

Pioneer of the Great Plains. Born here May 27, 1837. Assassinated at Deadwood August 2, 1876. Served his country as a scout and spy in the Western states to preserve the Union in the Civil War. Equally great were his services on the Frontier as express messenger and upholder of law and order. He contributed largely in making the West a safe place for women and children. His sterling courage was always at the service of right and justice. To perpetuate his memory this monument is erected by the State of Illinois.

A.D. 1929

3. *Wild Bill's birthplace, Troy Grove, Illinois. Constructed ca. 1836-37 by William Alonzo Hickok, the house was torn down in 1929 to make way for the memorial to Wild Bill, and the plot is now a state park. The woman and child in the photograph are unrelated to the Hickok family.*

4. *The only known portrait of William Alonzo Hickok, son of Otis and father of Wild Bill. Born on December 5, 1801, at North Hero, Grand Isle County, Lake Champlain, Vermont, William was a deeply religious man, but he taught his children to think for themselves and form their own opinions.*

He operated the first store in Homer (later renamed Troy Grove), Illinois, until the Panic of 1837 nearly ruined him. To support his family, he hired out as a plowman to local farmers until he was himself able to take up farming. That his family was never far from his thoughts is obvious from a letter he wrote in July, 1851, while visiting his mother in Union, New York. James especially was on his mind; he realized that his youngest son was afflicted by the same wanderlust that had prompted Oliver, his eldest, to leave home a few months earlier and go to California in the wake of the gold rush: "James," he wrote, "I shall hope to have a good account of you when I get home. Horace, I depend much upon you in my absence [and] hope you and James will be friendly & steady & stay at home as much as possible & do all you can for your Mother & be kind to the Girls."

On May 5, 1852, William Hickok died, leaving the management of the farm and home to his sons and daughters. (The letter from William to his wife and family is in the possession of Ethel Hickok, Troy Grove, Ill.)

5. *Polly Butler Hickok, Wild Bill's mother. The original of this photograph has not been found, but it is believed to have been made in the mid-1860s. Polly was born on August 4, 1804, in Bennington, Vermont (some sources say North Hero), and claimed as a distant relation the Civil War general Benjamin Butler. When William died, Polly was left the task of bringing up five children on her own, but by that time they were old enough to be of help to her. In her later years she worried a great deal about James and his exploits and followed his career with concern. For his part, James did his best to keep her well informed of his movements and made a practice of sending or bringing her expensive gifts. There was no criticism, but the family believed that money would have been better appreciated. When Polly learned of her son's terrible death, she suffered a physical collapse and mourned him until her own death two years later, in 1878. (Edith Andrews Harmon,* Pioneer Settlers of Troy Grove, Illinois, *58; Howard L. Hickok, "The Hickok Legend" [manuscript], 2.)*

6. *Oliver Hickok, the eldest of the Hickok children, born May 1, 1830, at Union, New York. When news of the gold strike in California reached Homer in 1849, Oliver announced his intention of joining the rush, but he was persuaded to wait until things settled down. Early in 1851, he set off for California with some other young men from the village and he spent the remainder of his life in that state, where he became well known as a breeder of fine horses. He was not, however, the owner of the celebrated trotting horse St. Julien (Orrin Hickok, the driver of that horse, has been mistaken for Oliver's own son Orrin, but they were unrelated).*

James kept in touch with Oliver. He was in Kansas when he learned that Oliver might pay a visit home and he promised to do the same once he knew when Oliver would be there. Oliver lost an arm in an accident, but it did not disrupt his career. A kind man, he appreciated poetry, and one of his signed visiting cards contains the following verse:

> Life should have higher, notable aims
> Than mirth, and song, and dance:
> O, men from sport and idle games,
> To higher deeds advance.

He died on June 29, 1898. (Harmon, Pioneer Settlers, *62-63.)*

7. *Lorenzo Butler Hickok from a carte de visite. Made between 1864 and 1868, this photograph shows an obvious resemblance between Lorenzo and the young James. Lorenzo was born on November 23, 1832, at Union, New York. In 1856 he accompanied James to Kansas but returned home when he learned that his mother was ill. In 1858 he was dispatched by the family to discourage James's romance with John Owen's daughter Mary, who was a half-blood Shawnee.*

By 1862, Lorenzo was employed as a wagon master in Missouri and Arkansas. Lorenzo was called "Tame Bill" because of his gentle manner and to distinguish him from his brother James, whom he saw infrequently. By the late 1860s he was employed as a wagon master in various frontier posts. In 1871 he returned to Troy Grove for good. Lorenzo never married, but he was popular with his neighbors and was generally called "Uncle Lon" by his family and the neighborhood children. He died in 1913. (Harmon, Pioneer Settlers, 64-65; Records of the Quartermaster General [1861-71], National Archives, Washington, D.C. Photograph courtesy Ethel Hickok.)

8. *Horace Dewey Hickok and his bride on their wedding day. Horace was born on October 5, 1834, at Bailey Point (now Tonica), Illinois. A quiet and cautious man, he did not share his brother James's spirit of adventure, and it is evident that during their childhood the brothers had their differences. He made several trips west to visit James, and even dreamed of owning a Kansas farm, but later decided he would be happier in Troy Grove. He remained there and was a farmer as well as a justice of the peace (a position he held from 1862 until 1916).*

Horace married Martha, the daughter of Robert and Ann Edwards, on February 1, 1867, but not until 1875 was the first of their eight children born. Martha was born on December 30, 1849, at Outwell, near Cambridge, England, and emigrated with

her parents when she was scarcely two years old. As a five-year-old girl she kissed James Hickok goodbye when, after promising that he would return and marry her, he set off for Kansas. As a very old lady she remembered him with great affection and told her own children many stories about him that, unfortunately, were rarely recorded.

In later years it was Horace who faced the unceasing demands from historians and others for details of the life of his brother James; occasionally he burst into print denouncing some particularly irritating nonsense. In 1900 he and his family moved from their farm to the town of Troy Grove, where he died in 1916. Martha died in 1932, and their unmarried daughter Ethel still lives in the old home. (Harmon, Pioneer Settlers, 72-74, 89-90. Photograph courtesy Ethel Hickok.)

9. *Photographs of Wild Bill's sisters in their youth have not yet come to light. This portrait of Celinda was made in her middle age. Born on September 3, 1839, she was called "Cindy" by the family. She married Erastus Dewey on January 3, 1867, and remained in Troy Grove until 1874, when she moved to Clay Center, Kansas. Erastus died in 1883, and Celinda later married a man named C. H. Smith. She died, following a fall, in Valley City, North Dakota, on November 8, 1916, and her body was brought back to Troy Grove for burial. Like her brothers and sister, she fought to preserve James's reputation, and her daughter Martha Dewey was largely responsible for exposing the alleged daughter of Wild Bill and Calamity Jane as an impostor. (Harmon,* Pioneer Settlers, *71.)*

10. *Born on October 29, 1842, Lydia Hickok was the youngest of the Hickok children. Family recollections suggest that she and James shared similar temperaments. The* Chicago Record, *December 26, 1896, reported that she had informed their reporter that "they always said that Bill [James] and I looked alike," and the newsman made a pointed reference to her "blue-gray eyes that have a steely glint to them." She married Harvey Stevenson on July 23, 1863. Marshall, their son, remembers meeting his "Uncle James" when he was five years old and asking him to shoot off his pistols to entertain him.*

Like her sister Celinda, Lydia lost her first husband. On December 12, 1874, she married James Hugh Barnes. The couple moved to Oberlin, Kansas, and later she became postmistress at Hooker, Kansas. In the early years of this century it was Lydia who refuted much of the nonsense written about her brother James and never ceased to be amazed at the myths that grew up about him. "Lyd" or "Aunt Lyd," as she was known to the family, served the communities in which she lived as a midwife and was much loved. She died on January 30, 1916. (Harmon, Pioneer Settlers, *71-72.)*

11.   *During the late 1840s and early 1850s, when the abolitionist movement was very strong, William Alonzo Hickok and some of his neighbors, who had friends among the Quaker settlement at Lowell, Illinois, took part in the highly dangerous business of helping runaway slaves. Some of the slaves were brought from Lowell to Troy Grove (by the river crossing at Utica) before heading on to Ottawa, Illinois, and further north. Runaway slaves occasionally remained at the Hickok home overnight or for several days until it was safe for them to move on. William built a secret cellar, where they were hidden. One of the runaways, a woman named Hannah, remained with the Hickok family for some years. She later moved to Malden, Illinois, where she married and settled down, but her last name is unknown. (Courtesy Ethel Hickok.)*

12. *Judge Samuel D. LeCompte, after whom Lecompton, Kansas, was named. When President Franklin Pierce established the territorial government of Kansas in the fall of 1854, he chose Andrew H. Reeder as its first governor and Daniel Woodson as secretary. The court was composed of LeCompte, Rush Elmore, and Saunders W. Johnston. In November there was an election for congressional delegates. Kansas was then launched into a bitter period of dispute between pro- and antislavery factions. A census revealed that there were about eighty-five hundred people on Kansas soil, and the question of slavery was put to a vote. Missouri Border Ruffians invaded and swamped the poll, to give the proslavery faction a resounding victory.*

By June, 1855, the Free Staters decided to hold a convention at Lawrence and repudiated the legislature, making freedom in Kansas their sole object. James H. Lane tried to subordinate the issue of slavery to other matters but failed, and slavery became the single issue. The battle for "Bleeding Kansas" was on.

LeCompte did little to disguise his proslavery views, and in May, 1856, his court at Lecompton indicted for treason many Free Staters and their leaders and issued warrants to the U.S. marshal for service. On May 11, 1856, U.S. Marshal Donalson issued a proclamation claiming that a deputy seeking to serve papers in Lawrence had been resisted. Proslavery men answered his call, and they marched on the town, which was generally believed to be a hotbed of antislavery sentiment. The armed men enabled the deputy to make his arrests, and then the mob sacked the town, burning down the newspaper offices and other important buildings. (William Frank Zornow, Kansas: A History of the Jayhawk State, 69-73. Photograph courtesy Kansas State Historical Society, Topeka.)

13.   *James H. Lane, the "Grim Chieftain of Kansas." He fought in the Mexican War of 1846-48 and was the leader of the radical arm of the Free State party. A belief in violent retaliation against the proslavery faction brought his Free State Army into bitter conflict with the Border Ruffians. Hickok is alleged to have been a member of Lane's army during 1857; legend asserts that Hickok paid the thirty dollars required for membership by means of a shooting match. Some writers have confused Lane's forces with the later "Red Legs" of Civil War fame.*

Lane later served as one of the state's first senators, and, following the Civil War, his career was marked by a succession of defeats in and out of Congress. A sick man, broken in health and spirit, he was brought home to Leavenworth where, on July 1, 1866, he shot himself through the head, lingering in agony until July 11. In its obituary the Emporia News *of July 14 remarked: "That he loved Kansas, and that Kansas loved him, is undeniable." (Zornow,* Kansas, *69-70. Photograph courtesy Kansas State Historical Society.)*

14.   *John Brown first came to Kansas in 1855 and was soon a leading figure among the abolitionists. A man tainted by hereditary insanity and dogged by repeated failures, he probably saw in the misery of Kansas a chance to prove himself or at least gain recognition. His hatred of the proslavery faction was so intense that it led him to the conviction that his deeds were divinely inspired. On May 23, 1856, he set off for Pottawatomie Creek, accompanied by four of his sons and three other men. There he murdered five proslavery men on May 24, leaving their bodies horribly mutilated, in an attempt to strike terror into the hearts of his enemies. The outcome was a border war.*

In 1859, Brown led an abortive attack on Harper's Ferry Arsenal. He was captured, put on trial, found guilty, and hanged on December 2, 1859. (Zornow, Kansas, 73-74. Photograph courtesy Kansas State Historical Society.)

15. *John Brown's murder of five men at Pottawatomie Creek (known as the Pottawatomie Massacre), and the border war that followed, involved federal troops who found themselves engaging both Free Staters and proslavery militants. Wilson Shannon, the recently appointed governor, resigned in August, 1856, and Daniel Woodson became the temporary governor. He declared that the territory was in open rebellion, and Lane's Free State Army prepared for a pitched battle with a "Grand Army" of Missourians that was advancing into the state, led by David R. Atchison (this army had engaged in a brief skirmish with John Brown). The anticipated battle was prevented by the arrival of United States troops from Leavenworth led by Colonel Philip St. George Cooke.*

John W. Geary took office as governor at Lecompton on September 11, 1856, and, with Cooke's help, he dissuaded Atchison from again entering Kansas. Meantime, on September 13, other federal troops fought a brief engagement at Hickory Point with a band of Free Staters led by Colonel James A. Harvey. The two-day battle left one man killed, nine wounded, and a number taken prisoner. James Hickok possibly acted as a scout for Harvey's command, for in a letter home dated November 24, he mentioned being with Harvey and that "thare is 29 of our company in custody at Lacompton yet. I have been out to see them once." He also added that his gun and horse had been supplied by a man on Crooked Creek and that, although roads, creeks, and springs between Lawrence and Lecompton were fairly scarce, there were plenty of land speculators around. He also noted that the new governor had little use for LeCompte and Donalson, a development that "caused . . . [some] excitement [among] the proslavery party but they know better than to make much fuss about it."

The illustration is from a watercolor by Samuel J. Reader and depicts the engagement at Hickory Point. (Zornow, Kansas, *75; for a complete copy of Hickok's letter see Rosa,* Wild Bill, *19-20. Photograph courtesy Kansas Historical Society.)*

16. *This specimen of Hickok's handwriting is a postscript to a letter written home from Kansas and dated November 24, 1856. Hickok's handwriting is well formed and even. A graphologist, ignoring the phonetic spellings (quite common at the time), expressed the opinion that James was well balanced and controlled, a strong-willed and intelligent individual who paid great attention to detail. (Courtesy Ethel Hickok.)*

17. *Israel B. Donalson, the first territorial U.S. marshal of Kansas, in old age. His proslavery views and unorthodox methods did not endear him either to Kansans or to the United States government. He resigned in November, 1856. (Courtesy Kansas State Historical Society.)*

18.
The original of this photograph of James Butler Hickok is a tinted tintype. It is enclosed in a gilt frame protected by glass and set in a leather case. Its clarity and detail are excellent. The photographer is unknown, but it is possible that it was made at Lawrence. In a letter to his family dated August 14, 1858, James promised that the next time he visited Lawrence he would have his picture taken: "I will send you my likeness and you can see whether it looks like a whisky face or not." On August 16, in a reference to his cousin Guy Butler's "awfull mustache and goatee," he declared: "I think my mustache and goatee lays over hisen Considerable. the fact of it is hisen ain't no Whare." The photograph has been reversed to correct the mirror image. (Rosa, Wild Bill, *24-26. Photograph courtesy Ethel Hickok.)*

32

33

19. *Guy Butler from a* carte de visite *credited to J. Harrison, Alton, Illinois, which has apparently been printed in reverse. The uniform has not been identified. A cousin of James Hickok, Butler joined him in Kansas for a brief period in 1858. On August 14, James wrote: "I have seen guy and like him first rate. he sings a little to[o] much about a man by the name of brown who wore two dangling curls. He stayed the first time he Came to see me three or fore days. Last Wednesday he Came to see me again and steyd [stayed] all day."*

In the same letter he remarked that he suspected Guy would advise the family that he was poor company because he remained silent for long periods. Later he noted that when Guy shaved it made him look "awfull thin" and, despite such leg-pulling, it is obvious that the pair got on extremely well and that James missed Butler when the latter returned to Illinois. (Rosa, Wild Bill, *23-24. Photograph courtesy Ethel Hickok.)*

20.   *Wild Bill in 1859.* This carte de visite, *bearing the imprint of Bowman &
Rawson, Peru, Illinois, came to light in 1976. It was in the possession of the son
of Fred Gibbs, who was related by marriage to the Hickoks. Fred Gibbs often helped
out during harvest and claimed that in 1859, after he visited Kansas and was returning
with James, who also was going to help with the harvest, they stopped off at La Salle,
where, after a haircut and a shave, they had their pictures taken.*

*The Hickok family has expressed the opinion that this photograph could be
either James or Horace. Examined under strong magnification, the figure, it was
concluded, was in fact James. Research by Edith Andrews Harmon, James's
grandniece, has revealed that photographers William Bowman and DeWitt S.
Rawson were established in Peru only during 1859, which adds credence to the
claims of both Gibbs and Charles Gross. Gross knew Wild Bill in Abilene and recalled
first meeting Hickok at Tiskilwa, Illinois, in 1859, when they both had helped with the
harvest. (Charles F. Gross to J. B. Edwards, January 26, 1926, Manuscripts Division,
KSHS; Rosa,* Wild Bill, *30-31.)*

21. *Fred Gibbs in middle age, from a tintype that has been reversed to obtain the correct image. The Gibbs family was related to the Hickoks after the marriage of Oliver Hickok's widow to Oliver Gibbs in 1814. Oliver Hickok was the son of Aaron and had died at Sackets Harbor, New York, during the War of 1812.*

Fred Gibbs recalled that when he was a young man he had visited James Hickok in Kansas, and, that in 1859 he had returned with James to Illinois. He said that they had their photographs taken at LaSalle, where they assisted with the family harvests. Fred ("Mac") Gibbs of Princeton, Illinois, Fred's son, told me shortly before his death that somewhere he still had the two original tintypes, but they have not yet come to light.

22. *It is claimed that in 1859, when James was employed by Russell, Majors and Waddell, he crossed the path of Joseph Alfred ("Jack") Slade. Slade was born about 1829 at Carlyle, Illinois, and served with the First Regiment, Illinois Infantry, during the Mexican War. Honorably discharged at Alton, Illinois, in October, 1848, he headed west for California but spent much of his time in Kansas, Colorado, and Utah territories.*

Only five feet six inches tall, with a dark complexion, black eyes, and light hair, Slade was a giant in reputation, and in some areas he was more feared than the Almighty. After a spectacular and controversial career, Slade was hanged by vigilantes following one of his drunken sprees at Virginia City, Montana, on March 10, 1864. Many regretted his death, for he was considered, in his sober moments, to be a good citizen with many redeeming qualities.

The illustration has long been disputed, for no actual photographs of Slade have come to light. A recent writer has reported that it was first discovered in the late 1930s or early 1940s and was the gift of a Mrs. G. L. Harris to the Pioneer Museum, Fort Collins, Colorado, on July 14, 1942. (Military Service Records Division, National Archives, Washington, D.C.; John B. McClerman, Slade's Wells Fargo Colt, 35. Photograph courtesy Montana Historical Society, Helena.)

23. *The company of Russell, Majors and Waddell was formed in 1855, and by 1860 this vast freighting concern also acquired mail contracts and had organized the Pony Express. They purchased the Leavenworth and Pike's Peak Express Company and John M. Hockaday's mail route from Saint Joseph to Salt Lake and Sacramento, promptly changing the name to the Central Overland California and Pike's Peak Express Company. The company recruited men experienced in handling mules as well as horses, for it was the mule more than the horse that was used to pull the stagecoaches and mud wagons that have become a part of western legend. A number of companies manufactured coaches, but the most famous was the Abbot-Downing Company of Concord, New Hampshire. Their famous "Concord" coaches, painted vermillion with yellow wheels and chassis, became a familiar sight. Original Concords are now hard to find; this one, named Guadalupe Pass, is an accurate reproduction made in 1965 by the Frizzell Coach and Wheel Works of Oklahoma City. (Frank A. Root and William E. Connelley,* The Overland Stage to California, *2, 153. Photograph Courtesy Frizzell Coach and Wheel Works.)*

THE STRUGGLE FOR LIFE.

24.   *This woodcut, a Western classic, is the work of Alfred R. Waud, the celebrated Civil War artist. It depicts Hickok dispatching four of the "M'Kandlas Gang" in an orgy of blood that has no equal in Western legend. (Harper's New Monthly Magazine, February, 1867, 284.)*

25. *David Colbert McCanles, the protagonist of the Rock Creek Tragedy, from a family portrait, circa 1859. Born on November 30, 1828, in Iredell County, North Carolina, he was the son of a village schoolteacher who was also a part-time fiddler and cabinetmaker. A brief period in a military academy convinced him that military life was not for him, and, gifted with great strength of body and mind, he sought his fortunes elsewhere. In 1859, while serving as sheriff of Watauga County, North Carolina, he disappeared with county funds and fled the state with Sarah Shull, the daughter of a millowner, leaving his wife and family to face the shame of his actions.*

McCanles stopped running at Rock Creek, Nebraska Territory, and there he purchased a small relay station, improved the water supply, and charged a toll of between ten and fifty cents a wagon on all vehicles crossing the creek on their way over the Oregon Trail. He later improved the property by building a new and better ranch on the east side of the creek. His wife and family later joined him, but the presence of Sarah led to frequent rows. (Rosa, Wild Bill, 34-52. Photograph courtesy Nebraska State Historical Society, Lincoln.)

26. *Sarah Shull, the twenty-six-year-old beauty of 1861, as a woman of mature
years. Born at Watauga River, Ashe County, North Carolina, on October 3, 1833,
she was the daughter of Phillip Shull and Phoebe Wand. Her relationship with
McCanles is a controversy in itself. The late Levi Bloyd believed that she was a
partner of McCanles, because he had seen two notes she held against him. The
1860 census, however, gives her age as twenty-six and her status as a "domestic."
Sarah was reticent about her relationship with Hickok, and following the shooting
she was sent east. She disappeared for a long time before turning up again at Shull
Mill, North Carolina, in 1897, where she remained until her death on June 1, 1932,
at the age of ninety-eight. Frank J. Wilstach interviewed her in 1925 but learned
little of what had happened at Rock Creek. She did intimate, however, that McCanles
was a confederate sympathizer and had intended to cause trouble when he visited
the station on that fateful day. Bloyd said that he was given two different accounts
of the story from two of Sarah's nieces. (Levi Bloyd,* Jefferson County History, Rock
Creek *[pages unnumbered]; Rosa,* Wild Bill, *40; Frank J. Wilstach,* Wild Bill Hickok,
68-71.)

27. *This photograph, made from a tintype, is alleged to be of Rock Creek at about the time of the Hickok-McCanles affray. A comparison of this photograph with an aerial photograph from the Nebraska State Historical Society suggests that it could indeed be the place but photographed some time after the incident. The coach depicted is a Concord, and I have found*

no evidence to suggest that the Russell, Majors and Waddell
Company was using Abbot-Downing vehicles in 1860-61. The
figure on the horse has not been identified. (Alan R. Ottley,
California Section Library, California State Library, to the
author, December 18, 1957. Photograph courtesy California
State Library, Sacramento.)

28. *The original handwritten documents from the Rock Creek hearing have been in the collection of the Nebraska State Historical Society since 1927. This document is important because it is one of several that refer to Hickok as "Dutch Bill," the name he was apparently known by at Rock Creek. The misspelling "Duch" may explain the name "Duck Bill," recently fastened upon Hickok by some writers eager to discredit him. As early as 1856, Hickok was called "Bill" or "William," and family recollections are that he also was called "Billy Barnes" (no one knows why) and "Shanghai Bill." That James was ever called "Shanghai Bill" is very doubtful. The "Shanghai Bill" of territorial days is believed to have been one William Hanschien, indicted under that alias by the territorial courts on charges of larceny. He may also have been the same man who, at the Lecompton constitution election on December 21, 1857, voted twenty-five times; he apparently copied the names of his "voters" from the Saint Louis business directory. (Case nos. 100-103, the* U.S. v. *William Hanschien alias Shanghai Bill,* Records of the First Territorial Court, Kansas, 1855-59, *Archives Division, KSHS; Manuscripts Division, NSHS. Photograph courtesy Nebraska State Historical Society.)*

CHAPTER TWO

Civil War Hero
(1861-1865)

The firing on Fort Sumter by Confederate forces on April 12, 1861, heralded the most tragic four years in American history—the Civil War. Loyalties were sometimes so divided that brother fought brother and father fought son. Few families escaped loss or involvement in the hostilities, and the Hickoks were no exception. While Horace remained behind at Troy Grove to run the family farm and manage its affairs, Lorenzo and James were in government service in southwest Missouri and parts of Arkansas.

James experienced his first major battle at Wilson's Creek, Missouri, on August 10, 1861. Horace recalled in later years that it almost scared the wits out of his younger brother when a hidden battery he was attempting to find suddenly opened fire. By October, however, both James and Lorenzo were employed as wagon masters and, during the next two years, saw each other infrequently.[1]

In a letter dated July 8, 1862 (the only one from this period that has so far come to light), written from Springfield, Missouri, James explained that he was unloading his ox trains and was expecting a difficult time ahead because General Samuel R. Curtis's supplies had been cut off. After a brief mention of family matters and a request that any reply be directed to him at Rolla, Missouri, he wrote that a local farmer had complained that Hickok's men had burned down his fence. James promptly offered to replace it, he said, and later to help "feed his corn for him," having convinced the farmer that he was as good a "Union man" as himself. The letter is signed "Capt. J. B. Hickok" (perhaps a courtesy rank extended to wagon masters).[2]

George Hance, a family friend who worked with the Hickok brothers during the early part of the war and who later knew them at Fort Riley, declared that, from the summer of 1862, James was called "Wild Bill" (for

45

an indeterminate reason) and, to distinguish him from James, Lorenzo was known as "Tame Bill."[3]

Some indication of Lorenzo's pacifist nature can be gleaned from his letters written from Rolla in 1863. He purchased a Colt Navy revolver for twenty-five dollars but sent it to Horace for safekeeping. Later he regretted his action but did not ask for its return. The revolver still survives, and it is a part of family legend that it originally belonged to James.[4]

Stories abound concerning Wild Bill's adventures during the war, and though most of them are obvious fiction, official records indicate that he was variously employed as a scout, a detective, and perhaps as a spy, which explains some of his more lurid adventures.[5]

Hickok is said to have been a spy attached to the Eighth Missouri State Militia, who spent many months behind Confederate lines, and a sharp-shooter at the Battle of Pea Ridge. Some verification of these claims can be found in contemporary accounts. The editor of the Leavenworth *Daily Conservative* remarked in his issue of February 1, 1867, that

> there has been a determined research in memory by those who partici-
> pated in the closing scenes of the war in North Arkansas. . . . and the
> result is that we knew Bill Hitchcock [sic] in 1864 and recognize his
> portrait in the [Harper's New Monthly] magazine for February. It is a fair
> representation for a wood cut. "Wild Bill," as he is called, rode in com-
> pany with the writer, and with Adjutant Mackle and Lt. Col. Hoyt from
> Newtonia, subsequent to the battle in October, to the Arkansas river,
> we think, but perhaps he remained at Fayetteville. . . . He came into
> Gen. Blunt's camp on the morning after the battle of Newtonia, having
> previously been with Price, and having spent several months in the
> camps in Arkansas, as stated in the article in question. . . . "Wild Bill"
> has made his mark in the war for the Union, and we accord him full
> credit for his risks and reward for results attained.

Hickok's miraculous escapes astride his magnificent mare Black Nell are still cited — as fact by some writers and as fiction by others. Another estab-lished part of his legend is his involvement with the Kansas guerrilla band known as the "Red Legs," but these stories are fictional.[6]

By the early months of 1865, short of food and equipment and faced with daily desertions, the Confederacy realized that it could not carry on. In Missouri its forces were dwindling, and spies reported daily on the troops' movements. On February 10, Hickok informed General John B. Sanborn,

"There are not more than ten or twelve rebels in any squad in the south-west that I can hear of." By April, Robert E. Lee, whose indomitable spirit and leadership had sustained all that remained of a once great army, realized that there was no point in suffering further hardship and bloodshed, and on April 9 he and General Ulysses S. Grant held their historic meeting at Appo-mattox Courthouse. Within days the news of the ending of the war spread across the plains, and one old-timer was adamant that it was Hickok who galloped by his wagon train as it approached Fort Zarah shouting, "Lee's surrendered!"[7]

In June the Union army prepared for demobilization. Among the first to go were the scouts and other civilian employees. By the end of the month Hickok was unemployed. He became a well-known figure on the streets of Springfield. For almost a month he occupied his time by gambling, and he and his companion, Davis Tutt, were a familiar sight, each armed with two revolvers. On the night of July 20 they fell out over a game of cards. Tutt reminded Hickok of a forty-dollar debt he owed him for a horse trade, which Hickok promptly paid. Then he claimed another thirty-five dollars. Hickok disagreed with this and pointed out that it was only twenty-five dollars, at which point Tutt took Hickok's prized Waltham repeater watch from the table. Tutt promised to wear the watch on the market square the next day, and Hickok threatened him with his life if he did. But Tutt defied him and, at about 6:00 P.M. on July 21, crossed the square. Hickok immediately walked toward him. When they were about one hundred paces apart, both men drew and fired, almost simultaneously. Tutt missed, but Hickok's ball took him through the heart.

Arrested on the orders of the military authorities, Hickok was charged with murder, but the charge was later reduced to manslaughter. At the trial on August 5 and 6, 1865, he was found not guilty, a verdict that aroused mixed reactions and some controversy in the local press. Still in Springfield in September, he ran in the election for town marshal and came in second of five candidates. In January, 1866, he witnessed a shooting and was called to give evidence. By then he was bored with Springfield, and he wasted no time obeying a request from his old friend and employer Captain Richard Bentley Owen to report to him at Fort Riley, Kansas.[8]

29.   *This tintype of Wild Bill was made about 1863 and has been reversed to obtain the correct image. Ethel Hickok informed the writer that her father, James's brother Horace, kept it in his desk for many years. "I remember as a small girl being shown the picture and dad telling me why he kept it there, but I have long since forgotten the reason."*

The original, only about two inches square, is mounted without glass in a guttapercha frame and shows the ravages of time.

The first official reference to Hickok's Civil War service is October 30, 1861, when he was engaged as a wagon master at Sedalia, Missouri, for one hundred dollars a month; his salary was later reduced to sixty dollars. He served in various parts of Missouri, particularly in the Rolla area.

From September, 1862, he was employed as a scout and perhaps as a spy. Stories of an association with the Kansas guerrilla band known as the Red Legs are without foundation. By 1864 he was employed as a special policeman, and later he was attached to Brigadier General John B. Sanborn's headquarters at Springfield, supplied with a horse and equipment, and paid five dollars a day. He was dropped from the roll of scouts on June 9, 1865, when the Union army began to demobilize. (Records of the Quartermaster General [1861-65]; Abstract Accounts, Third Auditor of Accounts of Captain R. B. Owen, A.Q.M., U.S.A., payments to J. B. Hickok [1864-65], National Archives, Washington, D.C. Photograph courtesy Ethel Hickok.)

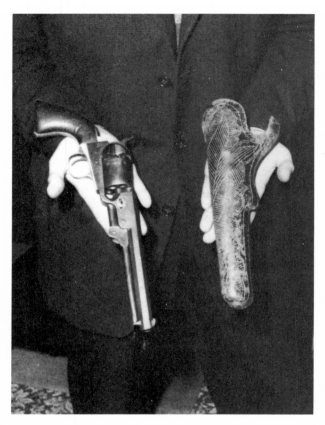

30. *The Colt 1851 model Navy revolver, with its original holster, that the Hickok family believed once belonged to Wild Bill, photographed on October 6, 1965. The holster was originally treated to a patent leather finish and is still in remarkably good condition. The pistol, however, has seen much neglect and has not fared so well. Horace Hickok told me that he had removed the mainspring many years earlier because "all the neighbor kids insisted on clicking Uncle Jim's gun and all but wore it out." The pistol, serial number 143098, was manufactured around 1863 and is one of the few fourth-model 1851 Navy revolvers that were fitted with dovetailed german-silver front sights. Standard weapons were equipped with a small brass pin. The pistol was not originally Wild Bill's but belonged to his brother Lorenzo, who had sent it to his brother Horace for safekeeping.*

31. *This boyish figure is George H. Hoyt. He made his name when he gave counsel to John Brown after Brown was imprisoned at Harper's Ferry. During the Civil War he became the third leader of the legendary Red Legs. Under his command they spread a reign of terror among Missouri "bushwackers" and the followers of Quantrill. When the band became ill-disciplined, however, General Blunt outlawed them, and many members joined other Kansas groups and regiments, among them Tough's "Buckskin Scouts." Hoyt served for a time as second-in-command in Colonel C. R. Jennison's Seventh Kansas Cavalry (known as Jennison's Jayhawkers). He was also responsible for the detectives attached to the Military District of the Border, Department of the Border. In August, 1863, the Fifteenth Kansas Regiment was formed, with Jennison in command and Lieutenant Colonel Hoyt as his second-in-command. Following the war Hoyt practiced law in Topeka. (Provost Marshal's Bureau, Scouts, Guides, Spies and Detectives [1861-66], National Archives, Washington, D.C.; Rosa,* Wild Bill, *66-68. Photograph courtesy Kansas State Historical Society.)*

32. *Lawrence, Kansas, as it appeared at the time of Quantrill's raid on August 21, 1863. Rumors of his intent were common for days before, but no real preparations were made to protect the town. Retaliation for Lane's raid on Osceola in 1861 was given as the reason for the attack, but other sources have said that Quantrill's raid was prompted by the collapse of a federal prison in Kansas City, in which some Confederate sympathizers were killed. An estimated three hundred men were with Quantrill when he attacked the town, setting fire to and destroying more than two hundred buildings, including the newspaper office, and killing nearly 150 people, many of them unarmed. Unknown to Quantrill, Lane was in town. He managed to escape Quantrill's forces and rally a pursuing force. Quantrill eluded them and fled to Missouri. (William E. Connelley,* Quantrill and the Border Wars, *411-17. Photograph courtesy Kansas State Historical Society.)*

33. *The buckskin-clad figure on the right in this photograph made around 1863 is William S. Tough. His buckskin suit is typical of the scout costume of the time. The fur collar is part of a cape shown spread across his shoulders. From his belt hang two Colt Navy revolvers in ornate open-topped holsters.*

Tough was every inch the frontiersman. Born on May 19, 1840, at Baltimore, Maryland, he was active in the Kansas-Missouri border war that immediately preceded the Civil War. In 1863 he was appointed chief of scouts of the District of the Frontier. When General Blunt outlawed the Red Legs, he organized a company of scouts to be attached to the Fourteenth Kansas, and Tough was appointed to lead them. These were the celebrated "Buckskin Scouts," whose exploits have frequently been confused with those of the Red Legs. After the war Tough settled down to a career in livestock, and for a short period in the 1870s he was U.S. marshal for Kansas. In 1900 he sold horses to the British army for use in the Boer War. He died, after a long and painful illness, on May 24, 1904, at Kansas City, Missouri. (Robert Schauffler, "Incidents in the Life of Captain William Sloan Tough," Manuscripts Division, KSHS. Photograph courtesy Kansas State Historical Society.)

34.   *Major General James G. Blunt, seated center, with his staff. Blunt commanded the Kansas District of the Union army's District of the Frontier and was responsible for the men employed as scouts and detectives in the District of the Border. By 1863, when the Red Legs had degenerated into a band of cutthroats, Blunt outlawed them but permitted those who wished to do so to enter the army or join the newly formed Fifteenth Kansas Regiment. (Courtesy Kansas State Historical Society.)*

35. *William Clarke Quantrill, from a photograph made during the Civil War. Born in Ohio in 1837, he taught school there for a time before moving to Utah and finally to Lawrence, Kansas, in 1859-60. His proslavery sympathies led him to Missouri, and soon he had organized a band of guerrillas that included some of the most noted cutthroats among the former Border Ruffians. By 1862 he and his men were accepted into the Confederate army, but the "Black Flag of Quantrill" still struck terror into the hearts of those who saw it: his new status and rank did not interfere with his cold-blooded slaughter of innocent and unarmed civilians. His attack on Lawrence was widely condemned, particularly by Colonel John Singleton Mosby, whose own guerrilla exploits as the South's foremost raider were as much admired as Quantrill's were reviled. The end of the Civil War, on April 9, 1865, meant little to Quantrill, and during a raid into Kentucky in May he was fatally wounded by federal troops. (For a complete review of Quantrill's career see Connelley, Quantrill. Photograph courtesy Kansas State Historical Society.)*

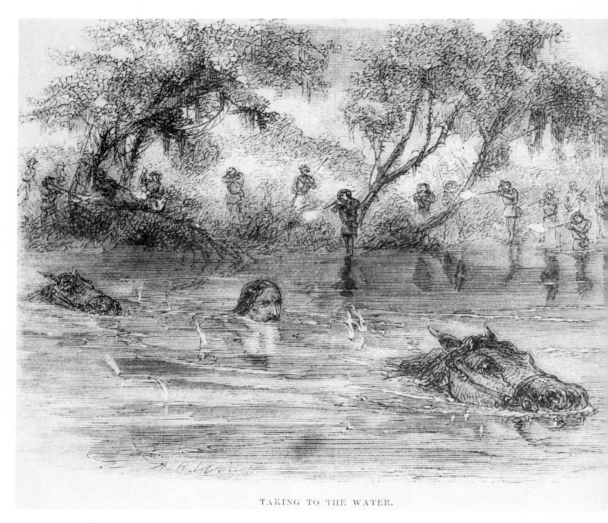

TAKING TO THE WATER.

36. *Another of Hickok's close shaves, according to Colonel George Ward Nichols. A. R. Waud drew this picture to depict Hickok's remarkable escape across a stream after being "suspicioned" by a Rebel companion. Although the bullets "zitted and skipped on the water," Hickok managed to reach the opposite bank in safety. Adventures such as this were given little credence by Hickok's contemporaries, but many of them enjoyed the stories just the same. (Harper's New Monthly Magazine, February, 1867, 282.)*

FOR LIFE OR DEATH.

37. Harper's *published this woodcut to illustrate the moment when Hickok and his scouting friend Tom Martin, chased by Confederate troops, made a dash to a wide ditch. Hickok's friend was shot from the saddle, but our hero sailed over the ditch and even managed to turn in his saddle and shoot dead two of his pursuers. Asked by the* Harper's *reporter Nichols why they had not slipped across in the dark, Hickok supposedly replied:*

> "Oh," said he, "mate and I wanted to show them cussed rebs what a Union soldier could do. We've been with them now for more than a month, and heard nothing but brag. We thought we'd take it out of them. But,"—and Bill looked across the green-sward to where his companion still lay motionless—"if they have killed my mate they shall pay a big price for it."

When the Harper's *story was published, the Springfield* Weekly Patriot *of January 31, 1867, announced to its readers: "Tom Martin . . . swore yesterday that Nichols' pathetic description of his untimely murder in 1863, in that article, was not true."* (Harper's New Monthly Magazine, *February, 1867, 278-79.)*

38. *General Sterling Price was born in Prince Edward County, Virginia, in 1809, and in his early years studied law. For some time he was involved in Missouri politics and favored that state's attempts to make Kansas a slave state. He entered the army in 1861 and accepted command of the reorganized state guard. His victory over General Nathaniel Lyon at Wilson's Creek won him immediate fame, but following the Confederate defeat at Pea Ridge, his state guard was integrated into the Southern army. Perhaps his most famous exploit was the "Price Raid of 1864," when he led a futile raid back into Missouri to gather recruits to divert Sherman's reinforcements at Atlanta. Hickok joined his forces as a spy and years later told Eugene A. Carr that on one occasion he had sat on his horse next to Price and the next day had ridden next to a Union officer, giving him the information he had obtained from Price.*

When the war ended, Price retreated to Mexico, but eighteen months later he returned to the United States. He died at Saint Louis, Missouri, in January, 1867. (Howard R. Lamar, ed., Reader's Encyclopedia of the American West, 965. Photograph courtesy Kansas State Historical Society.)

PUTTING UPON HIM.

39. *The fateful card game. Dave Tutt claimed that Wild Bill owed him thirty-five dollars, which Hickok denied. Tutt picked up Hickok's watch and promised to wear it on the square the next day. Ignoring the obvious danger to his health, Tutt marched onto the square on the evening of July 21, 1865. When the pair came face to face, there was no hesitation: both drew and fired, and Tutt missed. (*Harper's New Monthly Magazine, *February, 1867, 276.)*

"ARE YOU SATISFIED?"

40.   *Dave Tutt's friends were not eager to take on Hickok after he and Dave shot it out on the public streets of Springfield, Missouri, on July 21, 1865. Asked if he regretted killing Tutt, Hickok is reported to have replied: "I had rather not have killed him, for I want ter settle down quiet here now. But thar's been hard feeling between us a long while. I wanted ter keep out of that fight; but he tried to degrade me, and I couldn't stand that, you know, for I am a fighting man, you know." (Harper's New Monthly Magazine, February, 1867, 277-78.)*

41. *Albert Barnitz, dressed as captain of cavalry, from a photograph made at Leavenworth, circa 1868. Born on March 10, 1835, at Bloody Run, Pennsylvania, he was a noted poet and writer before the Civil War. During the war he served with distinction in the Second Ohio Volunteer Cavalry. Following Lee's surrender, the regiment was sent to Springfield, Missouri, where it performed policing duties. Barnitz actually witnessed the Hickok-Tutt shoot-out, and Hickok was arrested on his order. His version of the fight, recorded within hours of the event, corroborates much of the account of "Captain Honesty" (whose real name was Richard Bentley Owen) that appeared in* Harper's. *Barnitz's diary entry reads as follows:*

July 21, 1865　　Springfield, Mo.

"Wild Bill" the long-haired scout, shot "Tut," [*sic*] *tother* scout in the public square this evening [6 p.m.], killing him almost instantly. I had "Wild Bill" arrested at once, and turned him over to the civil authorities for trial. He is a noted scout, desperado and gambler, as was also the man who was killed. Both have been in the habit of appearing on the streets with two revolvers strapped on their belts. Both have been intimate for years and have been gambling together to-day. The ill will seems to have originated at the gambling table. "Tut" appropriating a watch which belonged to "Wild Bill," and refusing to give it up until a debt of $35 which he alleged was due him from "Wild Bill" was paid. "Wild Bill" desired him, thereupon, to distinctly understand that he ("Tut") couldn't walk the streets wearing his ("Wild Bill's") watch, but the motion was not heeded. Both fired simultaneously, as it appeared to me, at the distance of about 100 paces. "Tut" was shot directly through the chest. He was the son and support of a widow lady of this place.

　　On July 22, Barnitz noted: "'Wild Bill' has been released on bail. Public sympathy seems about equally divided between him and his victim."
　　When Barnitz later served as a captain in the Seventh Cavalry, he and Hickok were on very friendly terms. Barnitz was seriously wounded at the Battle of the Washita in November, 1868, and in 1870 retired from the army. He died on July 18, 1912. ("The Diary of Major Albert Barnitz," [manuscript], Beinecke Library, Yale University, copy supplied by Robert M. Utley; Robert M. Utley, Life in Custer's Cavalry. 3, 37-38, 247; Joseph G. Rosa, "George Ward Nichols and the Legend of Wild Bill Hickok," Arizona and the West, vol. 19, no. 2 [Summer, 1977], 135-62. Photograph courtesy Beinecke Rare Book and Manuscript Library, Yale University, New Haven, Conn.)

BLACK NELL.

42. *Black Nell, very much a part of the Hickok legend. Nichols reported that Hickok had said to him, "Black Nell has carried me along through many a tight place." Because of his careful training she had saved his life on many occasions, and to demonstrate her complete obedience he persuaded her to climb onto a billiard table in Ike Hoff's saloon. When she stepped down, he sprang upon her back and cleared the sidewalk and a flight of steps at a single bound, landing in the street.*

The editor of the Springfield Weekly Patriot, *however, declared on January 31, 1867, that she was not a mare but a stallion, blind in one eye but a "goer," and had Bill actually attempted such a leap*

he would have got a severe fall in the doorway of the barroom, *sure,* to make no mention of clearing at 'one bound' a porch twelve feet wide, and five feet high, a pavement twelve feet, and half the width of the roadway, (twenty-five feet by actual measurement) making a total of forty-nine feet, without computing any margin inside the room from which she (or he) "bounded."

*Black Nell is reported to have been purchased by Hickok from the army during the war, and to have died at Kansas City in 1869, greatly mourned, but no evidence has been found to verify either claim. (*Harper's New Monthly Magazine, *February, 1867, 280; William E. Connelly,* Wild Bill and His Era, *70; Wilstach,* Wild Bill Hickok, *106.)*

THE FAREWELL.

43.   *When George Ward Nichols left Springfield, he shook hands with Wild Bill and asked if he could publicize a few of Hickok's adventures. "Certainly you may," Hickok replied, "I am sort of public property." But Hickok, with tears in his eyes, wanted Nichols to assure him that his "old and feeble" mother back in Illinois would read nothing to suggest that he was a cutthroat or a vagabond: "I'd like her to know what'll make her proud. I'd like her to hear that her runaway boy has fought through the war for the Union like a true man."*

How much of Hickok's speech to Nichols was sincere and how much of it was leg-pulling may never be known, but he did concern himself with reassuring his family that he was safe and well. Nichols, of course, kept his word. In a footnote he declared that his tale of Hickok's adventures had been verified by many witnesses, and that he had "no doubt of its truth." (Harper's New Monthly Magazine, February, 1867, 285.)

44.   *When* Harper's *published this woodcut of Hickok as the frontispiece of Nichols's "Wild Bill" article, the editor of the Springfield* Weekly Patriot *remarked on January 31, 1867: "The portrait . . . is a most faithful and striking likeness—features, shape, posture and dress—in all it is a faithful reproduction of one of Charley Scholten's photographs of 'Wild Bill.'" One of the surviving granddaughters of Charles Scholten informed me that no photographs of Wild Bill were retained by the family. John Scholten, their grandfather's brother, of Saint Louis, Missouri (who photographed Custer several times), was the better known of the two, having won prizes for his work.*

Alfred R. Waud drew the original plate from which the woodcut was made, and that Hickok's coat is buttoned up the wrong side suggests it was copied directly from a tintype and is therefore in reverse. The holstered pistol may have been added for effect, but only an examination of the original plate (if it exists) would resolve the matter. The plate was made circa 1864-65.

WILD BILL.

45. *Colonel George Ward Nichols, who more than anyone else promoted the Hickok legend, from a woodcut taken from a photograph and published in* Harper's Weekly, *September 26, 1885. Born in Main in 1831, Nichols spent many years in Boston, where he became a journalist. In the late 1850s he went west to Kansas to report on the struggle there, and later he worked as art editor for the New York* Evening Post *and contributed articles to other magazines.*

Nichols was commissioned a captain in the Union army on April 26, 1862, and became an aide to Major General John C. Frémont. Later he was an aide to Major General William T. Sherman and was with him when he marched through Georgia and took Atlanta. In 1865, Nichols published The Story of the Great March: From the Diary of a Staff Officer.

Nichols's article in Harper's *on the exploits of Wild Bill was unjustifiedly condemned by later writers; only now is it known that much of what he wrote was true or in part based on fact. At the time of his death from tuberculosis on September 15, 1885, at Cincinnati, Ohio, he was the respected founder and president of the College of Music in that city. (Dictionary of American Biography, vol. 13, 494; Cincinnati Enquirer, September 16, 1885.)*

46.
Published versions of this photograph are variously dated. I tentatively dated it about 1868 in the 1974 edition of They Called Him Wild Bill, *but a close examination of the original* carte de visite *has led me to a change of opinion and date. Hickok's hair is shorter than it was in later photographs, and, disregarding some retouching on the moustache (made on the plate from which the print was made and not on the print), the face bears a strong resemblance to the 1863 portrait. But it is his dress that prompted me to compare the photograph with the* Harper's *woodcut. The jacket and trousers in both photographs appear to be identical, and the hat bears a resemblance to the one shown in the woodcut. The original* carte de visite *bears the imprint "A. Neuman, Photograph & Ambrotype Artist, Rolla, Mo." An examination of existing city directories from 1863 to 1869 showed no evidence of Neuman, and I have come to the conclusion that either he was an itinerant or had copied the photograph at a later period. If, as I suspect, Neuman was not the original photographer, then perhaps this is a copy of a missing Scholten original and was made about 1864-65 rather than in 1868. (Courtesy Kansas State Historical Society.)*

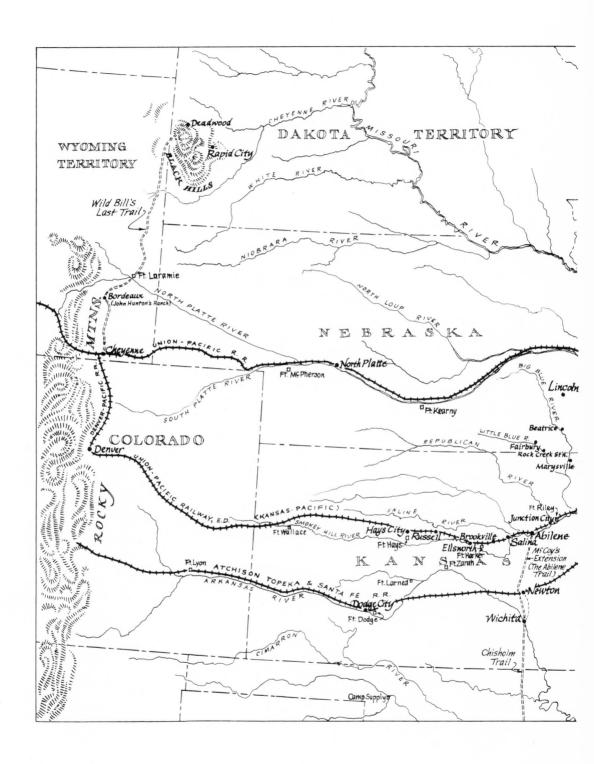

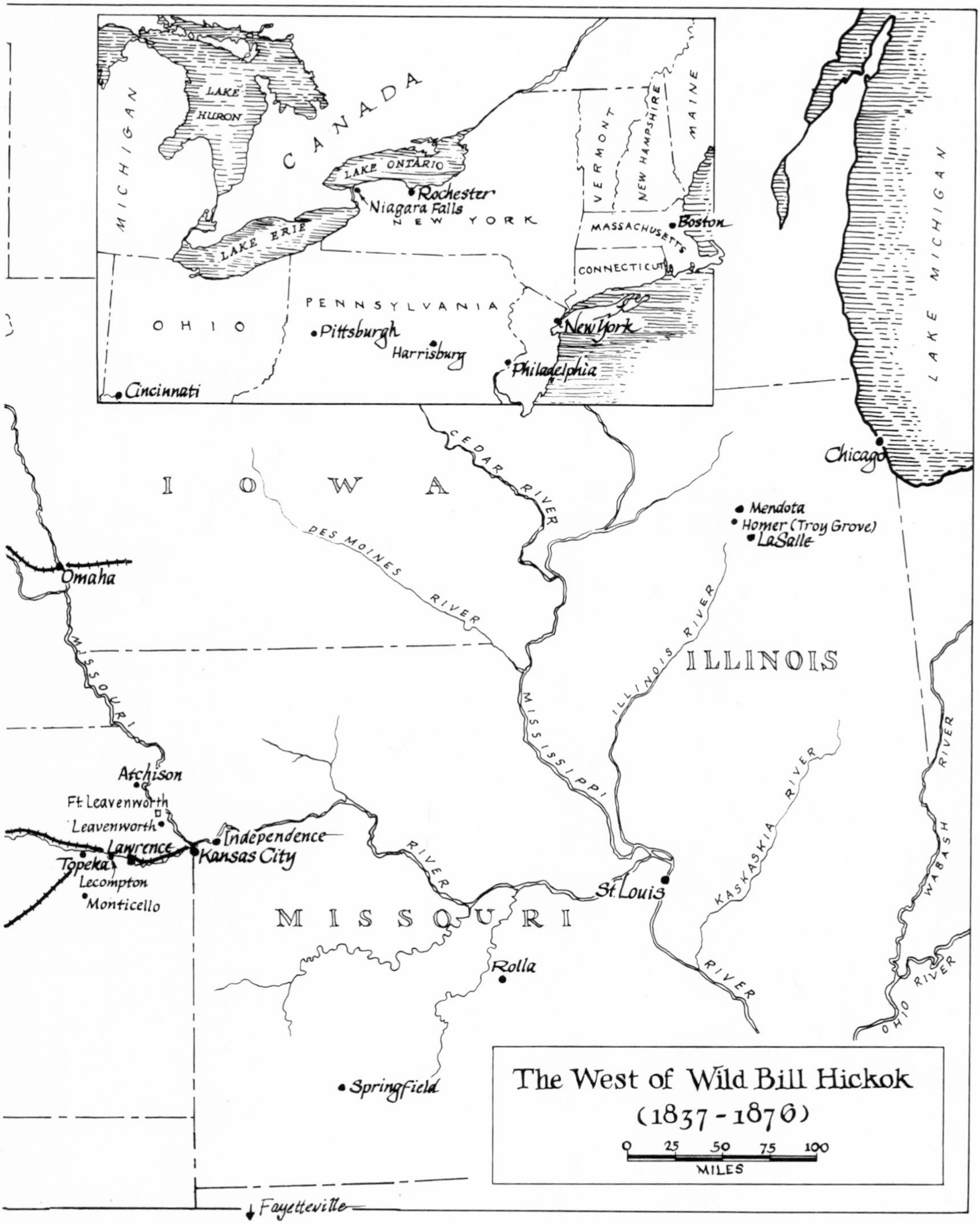

The West of Wild Bill Hickok
(1837 - 1876)
0 25 50 75 100
MILES
CANADA
LAKE HURON
MICHIGAN
LAKE ONTARIO
LAKE ERIE
Rochester
Niagara Falls
NEW YORK
VERMONT
NEW HAMPSHIRE
MAINE
MASSACHUSETTS
Boston
CONNECTICUT
PENNSYLVANIA
OHIO
Pittsburgh
Harrisburg
New York
Philadelphia
Cincinnati
IOWA
CEDAR RIVER
DES MOINES RIVER
LAKE MICHIGAN
Chicago
Mendota
Homer (Troy Grove)
LaSalle
ILLINOIS
ILLINOIS RIVER
MISSISSIPPI
KASKASKIA RIVER
WABASH RIVER
OHIO RIVER
Omaha
MISSOURI
Atchison
Ft. Leavenworth
Leavenworth
Lawrence
Topeka
Lecompton
Monticello
Independence
Kansas City
RIVER
MISSOURI
St. Louis
Rolla
Springfield
Fayetteville

CHAPTER THREE

Plainsman
(1866-1869)

At the end of the Civil War attention again was focused on the frontier. During the war years the Indians had taken advantage of the conflict to pursue their own claims to the territory that made up the frontier. As white emigrants again turned toward that western territory, it became obvious that the army would once more be called upon to protect them.

At Fort Riley, Kansas—a jumping off place for emigrants heading west and a base for a large number of underpaid and disillusioned soldiers of the frontier army—the authorities had their work cut out for them keeping tempers cool and the men fully employed. Hickok reached the post in late February or early March, 1866, and he was hired by Captain R. B. Owen as a guide, with the added responsibility of "hunting up Government property."[1] Legend asserts that Hickok was also appointed as a deputy U.S. marshal at this time, but this is not borne out by available records.

Hickok's appearances in and around the fort during 1866 were intermittent. In May he was detached from the post to act as a guide for General William Tecumseh Sherman, who was then on a guided tour of the West.[2] Hickok left Sherman's command at Fort Kearny, Nebraska Territory, where he was promptly hired as a "scout and guide" by Colonel James F. Meline, who was himself attached to General John S. Pope's expedition en route to Santa Fe, New Mexico. Hickok possibly accompanied the tour all the way to Santa Fe, for post returns confirm that he was absent from there between May and September and had accumulated $225 in back pay.[3]

In July, 1866, Congress authorized four new cavalry regiments to be numbered seven through ten. The Seventh was organized at Fort Riley late in August, but it was December before the regiment was up to strength, by which time its new lieutenant colonel, George Armstrong Custer, had arrived to assume command of both the regiment and Fort Riley.[4]

Sometime during 1866, Wild Bill renewed his acquaintance with Jack Harvey, well known in guerrilla circles as "Captain" Jack, whom he had met during the late war. Harvey's postwar activities are unknown, although it was generally understood that he was Hickok's "partner." Perhaps the first recorded reference to their plains partnership was made early in January, 1867, when the pair swore out a complaint against John Tobin and William Wilson following the theft of two mules from Fort Riley. By the time the case came to trial, both Hickok and Harvey were out on the plains with the army.[5]

By 1867, Indian unrest was causing increasing alarm, both in Washington and on the plains, where outlying settlements were under attack from isolated bands of warriors. The government decided that action was needed. General Sherman, in command of the Division of the Missouri, ordered Major General Winfield Scott Hancock, a soldier with a distinguished Civil War record and the commander of the Department of the Missouri, to organize a force to march into Indian country in an effort either to persuade the Indians to accept peace terms or to crush them.

In April, during the early stages of the campaign, Wild Bill appeared at Fort Zarah, where he met the *Harper's Weekly* artist Theodore Davis. Davis was unimpressed by the man who only two months before had been the subject of a lead article in the paper's monthly edition and did his best to avoid him. Another journalist traveling with the command reacted quite differently. Henry M. Stanley, the Welsh-born reporter for the Saint Louis *Democrat*, was fascinated by Hickok and devoted much space to him.[6]

Hancock's army was made up of six companies of the Seventh Cavalry, seven companies of the Thirty-seventh Infantry, and a battery of the Fourth Artillery Battalion—about fourteen hundred men in all. Records show that Hickok was employed between January and April as a wagon master, but from May 1, on the personal orders of General Hancock, he was listed and paid as a scout at one hundred dollars a month and assigned to the Seventh Cavalry.[7]

Hancock's Indian War, as it was scathingly called, was a disaster. Far from convincing the Indians of the army's peaceful intentions, it threw many of them into panic and desperate flight. A number of civilians were murdered, and settlements were burned. Following weeks of fruitless pursuit, during which time Hancock incurred the enmity of many of his officers, in particular of Custer, a council was arranged between the army and the Indians at Fort Dodge, and a semblance of peace was restored.

Hickok's engagement with the army was over in August, during which month he spent twenty-one days in carrying dispatches and in other duties. By the early fall he was employed as a deputy U.S. marshal, a position he was to hold sporadically until late in 1870.[8]

During the latter part of the year he and Jack Harvey were often seen together in and around Fort Harker, and an undated and as yet unidentified newspaper clipping discloses that the pair were not averse to reckless displays of nerve—Harvey once put a ball through Hickok's brand-new watch, and, in reprisal, Hickok parted Harvey's hair with a bullet.[9] Jack Harvey died at Ellsworth on March 13, 1868, the victim of tuberculosis. Hickok's reaction to his death is not known, for he was never heard to discuss it. It is possible, however, that Hickok trusted and shared his friendship with this man even more than with Cody, whom he had known much longer.[10]

During most of the early months of 1868, Hickok was active in his role of deputy U.S. marshal and also as the subject of newspaper gossip. Later, as the summer drew to a close, the Indians were again on the attack, and, on August 18, Hickok signed on as a guide for the Tenth Cavalry. Reengaged by the same regiment in September, he remained with them all through the winter months of 1868-69.[11]

When General Philip H. Sheridan launched a winter campaign against the Indians in 1868, he did so in the belief that the tribes would not expect such a move. On November 27, Custer attacked the Cheyenne chief Black Kettle's camp on the Washita and killed an estimated 103 Indians, including women and children, and captured their pony herd and about 53 women and children. Hickok was not present during this action. He was with General Penrose's command, snowed in on Palo Duro Creek, where he remained until the command was joined by General Eugene A. Carr and the Fifth Cavalry. Cody was Carr's scout, and he and Hickok were reunited in a "jollification" of stolen beer. The antics of the pair became a constant source of irritation, for Carr disliked Hickok and did his best to keep them apart.[12]

At the end of the campaign Wild Bill and the army finally parted. There is some evidence to support the belief that he was wounded by a lance when he met a number of Cheyennes while carrying dispatches between Forts Lyon and Wallace; his sister recalled that a leg wound received in such an encounter became infected. News that his mother was ill, coupled, perhaps, with a desire for a change of scene, prompted him to head eastward to Troy Grove.[13]

JUNCTION CITY KANS. 1866

47. *The photographer who made this view of Junction City in 1866 has not been identified, but it may have been R. C. Whitney, who took over the business of Carter and Brother. The Carters had made a number of photographs of the fort, the local people, and the surrounding area. Whitney moved to Junction City in April, 1866, to a place on Washington Street, but his movements after that can not be traced. One Meixel, another local photographer, is credited with photographs of Mrs. Custer, but, like those of Whitney, few of his photographs have been identified.*

Wild Bill was a frequent visitor to Junction City between 1866 and 1871, and it was alleged in 1876 that in 1867 he had kept a saloon and gambling "hell" on Seventh Street, but the story is not substantiated. Old-timers recalled his gambling and his habit of entertaining townspeople with displays of his pistol skill. He shot coins from fence posts; he shot at stable rats or quail; and occasionally he gave impromptu demonstrations in the stable yard of the Empire Hotel or at Callen's livery stable, with a six-shooter in either hand. (Captain W. F. Pride, U.S.A., The History of Fort Riley, 155-56; Percy G. Ebbutt, Emigrant Life in Kansas, 12-13. Photograph courtesy Kansas State Historical Society.)

707 BROADWAY, N.Y

48. *George Armstrong Custer, "the boy general," from a photograph credited to Mora of New York, circa 1872. Born at New Rumley, Ohio, on December 5, 1839, he entered West Point in 1857. His natural dash and verve and a personal courage beyond question earned him rapid promotion, and by the end of the war he was the youngest general in the United States Army.*

Under Custer's command the Seventh Cavalry achieved a fame that is now legendary. Although a substantive lieutenant colonel, he retained the brevet rank of major general from the war and was entitled to be called "General."

He greatly admired courage and was particularly taken with Hickok and William Comstock, devoting much space to them in the articles he published in Galaxy Magazine *in 1872 that were reproduced in 1874 in his book* My Life on the Plains. *He described Wild Bill as a "strange" character, just the one which a novelist might gloat over. . . . a Plainsman in every sense of the word, yet unlike any other of his class." Hickok, a scout and courier for the Seventh during the summer of 1867, was also a favorite of Mrs. Custer.*

By 1875, Custer's involvement in politics had begun disturbing President Grant. Only the pleads of Generals Sheridan, Sherman, and Terry persuaded the president to allow Custer to accompany the Little Bighorn expedition. On June 25, 1876, Custer and two companies of the Seventh were annihilated in the greatest defeat the United States Army ever suffered at the hands of the Indians. Custer's "last stand" remains one of the most controversial incidents in frontier history. (Lawrence A. Frost, The Custer Album, *17ff, 148-74. Photograph courtesy Herb Peck, Jr.)*

49.   *Elizabeth Bacon Custer and the general, from a retouched tintype made about 1865. Born on April 8, 1842, at Monroe, Michigan, "Libbie" Custer was one of the most beautiful women of her time. She was devoted to George Custer and spent the thirty-four years she survived him in preserving his fame. In her books and letters she described in great detail the people she knew and what life was like on the plains. Of Wild Bill she wrote:*

Physically, he was a delight to look upon. Tall, lithe and free in every motion, he rode and walked as if every muscle was perfection. . . . He was rather fantastically clad, of course, but all that seemed perfectly in keeping with the time and the place. He did not make an armoury of his waist, but carried two pistols. He wore top-boots, riding breeches, and dark blue flannel shirt, with scarlet set-in front. A loose neck-hankerchief left his fine, firm throat free."

Shortly before her death on April 6, 1933, just two days before her ninety-first birthday, Libbie said that she had only two regrets in her long life: her husband's death, and the fact that she had "no son to bear his honored name." (Lawrence A. Frost, General Custer's Libbie, *12, 13; Elizabeth Bacon Custer,* Following the Guidon, *160-61. Photograph courtesy W. H. Edwards.)*

50. *Thomas Ward Custer. Born at New Rumley, Ohio, on March 15, 1845, he idolized his older brother George and shared with him a love of adventure and practical jokes. During the Civil War, Tom became a hero in his own right, winning two Medals of Honor, the only person in any branch of the service to do so. He was appointed a first lieutenant in the regular army on July 28, 1866, and spent the remainder of his military service with his brother's Seventh Cavalry Regiment. In this photograph, made in the late 1860s, he wears both Medals of Honor. A close examination shows that the original photograph was retouched—to cut down the reflection from the studio lighting—making Tom's light blue eyes look darker than they really were.*

It has been alleged that Hickok once arrested Tom when he was drunk in Hays, Kansas, and that in revenge Tom sent in a number of troopers with orders to kill him, but there is no evidence to support this story. Had Tom really had a grievance against Wild Bill, it would have been more in character for him to have sought him out himself. Although Tom never married, his charm and wit made him a great favorite with the ladies. He died with his brother at the Little Bighorn on June 25, 1876. His body was later recovered, and he is now buried in the military cemetery at Leavenworth, Kansas. (Frost, Custer Album, *18, 76, 156-57.)*

51. *This self-portrait of Theodore R. Davis was published in* Harper's Weekly *in 1867 to accompany the artist's articles and illustrations of the Hancock expedition. His two Colt 1860 Army revolvers are worn, butts forward, in the approved plains manner, and in his hand is his favorite Ballard rifle. His "uniform" is also typical of the period.*

Born in 1840, Davis joined Harper's *in 1861 and covered most of the major Civil War actions. His reports and sketches of the Hancock War were widely read. He made little mention of Wild Bill in his reports, but in one of the several manuscripts that came to light following his death in 1894 was a detailed comment on Hickok, whom he actively disliked. He recalled that Hickok was "by nature a dandy" and launched into a description of him that is not borne out by other contemporary accounts.*

Despite his extraordinary, dandylike apparel, Wild Bill lived up to his reputation for courage by leading an expedition to capture some deserters. He insisted on going alone to their hideout in an attempt to persuade them to surrender. (For Davis's "pen picture" of Hickok see Elmo Scott Watson, ed., and Theodore R. Davis, "Henry M. Stanley's Indian Campaign in 1867," Westerners' Brand Book, *vol. 2 [1945-46].)*

52.   *Henry Morton Stanley from a* carte de visite *by Maull and Fox, London, circa
1871-75. Stanley was born at Denbigh, Wales, on January 28, 1841, the illegitimate
son of John Rowlands and Elizabeth Parry. He was deeply affected by the circumstances
of his birth, which shamed him for most of his life. He ran away from home in his
teens and emigrated to the United States, where he was befriended by Henry Hope
Stanley, whose name he adopted; "Morton" was added at a later date. Stanley had
the unusual experience of serving on both sides during the Civil War. He then spent
some time in the Middle East before he reappeared in Kansas in 1867, where he
reported on the Hancock expedition for the* Weekly Missouri Democrat. *He met Hickok
at Fort Zarah early in April, 1867, and filed a "pen picture" of Wild Bill that is, if
highly colored, in part truthful. Unlike Theodore Davis, Stanley found Hickok a
fascinating character, and in his later years he enthralled friends and after-dinner
guests with stories of the man and his own experiences in the "Wild West."*

 *Stanley's later career included expeditions into Africa and a growing reputation
as an explorer, for which he was later knighted. But his greatest fame came in 1871
when, with the backing of James Gordon Bennett of the New York* Herald, *he set
out to find David Livingstone. His greeting when the two finally met ("Dr. Livingstone,
I presume?"), is one of the world's best-known quotations. He died on May 10, 1904.
(Richard Hall,* Stanley: An Adventurer Explored, *99, 152, 172, 353; Rosa,* Wild Bill,
111. Photograph courtesy Royal Geographical Society, London.)

53. *Ellsworth, Kansas, in the summer of 1867. With the growing violence and the increasing number of saloons and gambling houses, the citizens decided that law and order was a priority. On August 10, Ellsworth held its first election. Wild Bill was defeated in the race for marshal; the voters elected Chauncey B. Whitney as township constable and Captain E. W. Kingsbury as county sheriff. In the November election for county offices, Wild Bill stood for sheriff and polled 155 votes (the largest number within city limits), but he received few votes from outside the city, and Kingsbury was again elected.*

A curious letter from one Jas. B. Comstock (whom some think may have been Hickok) appeared in the November 11, 1867, issue of the Saint Louis Weekly Missouri Democrat. It stated that Wild Bill, who was the "radical candidate for sheriff of Ellsworth county, and received the full support of the party—was only destined to suffer the fate of his ticket which was defeated by only a very small majority, but to bloom and blossom again at an early day." (Rosa, Wild Bill, *116-18. Photograph courtesy Kansas State Historical Society.)*

54. *The depot at Ellsworth, photographed by Alexander Gardner in September, 1867. The vehicle in front of the depot is a concord mud wagon of the type that plied between places so small that they did not justify regular stagecoach stops. In the back a number of freight wagons can be seen. (Courtesy Kansas State Historical Society.)*

55a–c *(pages 81-83). By 1867, Leavenworth boasted several photography studios, among them the Nobles Gallery and E. E. Henry's Gallery at 42 Delaware Street. Henry was considered "by far the best artist in the City," and sometime in 1867 or 1868, Wild Bill was persuaded to sit for him. Until recently it was assumed that this photograph was a bust portrait, but in 1972 I found a version of it published in an unnamed 1920s magazine showing that the original was a portrait of three-quarter*

b

length. Subsequent correspondence with David R. Phillips, the owner of the original plate at the time, and a personal opportunity to examine it, revealed that Hickok wore his waistcoat and shirt partly undone (see also Plate 56b). A fine watch chain hangs down to an ornate fob, and around his waist is a pleated silk sash or cummerbund. Facial blemishes and freckles are clearly evident, and this print is reproduced as 55c,

82

c

with no attempt at retouching. The original glass plate measures 4³⁄₁₆″ x 3⅛″. For comparison, see Plate 55a, the 1960 retouched version sold by Mary Everhard, and 55b, the softer but unretouched version of 55c that she later provided for publication. The original plate is now owned by the Amon Carter Museum. (Plates 55a and b courtesy the late Mary E. Everhard; Plate 55c courtesy the Amon Carter Museum, Fort Worth, Texas.)

56a–c *(pages 84-85).* Wild Bill was a frequent visitor to Topeka, and he was photographed there on several occasions. Until recently, however, little was known of these photographs or of who made them. But some information came to light in the Topeka State Journal *of January 1, 1898: in publicizing the discovery of the only known "authentic" photograph of Wild Bill, then in the possession of a man named George Wolff, an early-day livery stable owner, the paper published a woodcut of it (56a) and stated that Hickok himself had given it to Wolff in 1866 and that the original had been made by a man named Smith. One other photograph of Hickok is credited to Charles T. Smith, and a search of old city directories showed that he had practiced on Kansas Avenue between 1866 and 1868 or 1869 and then disappeared. A print of the original Smith portrait is shown as Plate 56b, and a later vignette, retailed and sold by W. Ames, 189 Kansas Avenue, is reproduced as 56c.*

Wolff's dating of 1866 was erroneous, for it is evident that the portrait dates from 1867 or 1868. Here, as in the Henry portrait, Hickok wears his waistcoat open and his shirt partly unbuttoned (the lower pleat looks almost like a pistol butt). This is perhaps Hickok's most "dressed up" portrait. The jeweled collar stud and the "wire-held" wing collar make him very fashionable. According to the Leavenworth Daily Times, *December 27, 1925, Wolff's daughter Mary presented the original Smith photograph to William E. Connelley, but it, like so many other priceless items in his possession, cannot be traced after 1930, when Connelley died. (Plates 56a and c courtesy Kansas State Historical Society.)*

57. *Fort Larned, Kansas, from a pencil sketch by Theodore Davis published in Harper's Weekly, June 8, 1867. Fort Larned, considered one of the most important posts on the central plains, was situated on the Pawnee Fork some fifteen miles from its confluence with the Arkansas River. The fort was established in October, 1859, and named after Paymaster General Benjamin F. Larned. Its soldiers guarded the Santa Fe Trail during the white-Indian hostilities of 1861 to 1868. It was also the administrative center for the Indian Bureau's Cheyenne and Arapaho Agency. Abandoned in 1878, it is now a national historic site. (Courtesy Kansas State Historical Society)*

58. *Infantry as well as cavalry had a part to play on the frontier. Here Company C of the Third Infantry Regiment poses at Fort Larned in 1867. (Courtesy Kansas State Historical Society.)*

59a, b *(pages 88-89). The publication of Nichols's "Wild Bill" article in* Harper's New Monthly Magazine *prompted Robert M. De Witt to include two Wild Bill adventures in his series of 1867, thereby making of Hickok a dime novel hero before Buffalo Bill Cody. It was in December, 1869, that Ned Buntline (E. Z. C. Judson) publicized Cody in Buffalo Bill, King of the Bordermen in the* New York Weekly. *Hickok's reaction to Buntline, who had him killed off in the story, was predictable: "Ned Buntline has been trying to murder me with his pen for years; having failed, he is now, so I am told, trying to have it done by some Texans, but he has signally failed so far." This allusion to Texans was in reference to reports circulating in 1873 that Hickok had been murdered, but he hastily reassured his friends and the press that he still lived.*

The cover of De Witt's Ten Cent Romances, *no. 3 ("Wild Bill, Indian Slayer") was copied from the* Harper's *story, but the cover for no. 10 ("Wild Bill's First Trail") was more typical of the dime novel of the period. In both issues Hickok was depicted saving damsels from fates worse than death and bringing to an end the careers of assorted bad men. In the second story, however, more emphasis was placed on his*

Monthly.]   [Number. 3.

DE WITT'S TEN CENT
ROMANCES

Wild Bill, the Indian Slayer

FOR SALE BY
R. M. DE WITT, Publisher,
13 FRANKFORT STREET, N.Y.

a

exploits as a scout, Indian fighter, buffalo hunter, trapper, and guide, with a hint that
it was "told by himself" and therefore more entertaining than any "mere work of
fiction could possibly be."

When copies of these publications reached Kansas, Hickok had his leg pulled but

took it in good humor. One editor noted that Hickok remained in Hays "probably engaged in preparing his LIFE for De Witt." (Mendota [Ill.] Bulletin, April 11, 1873; Leavenworth Daily Conservative, December 14, 1867. Photographs courtesy Library of Congress.)

60. *The cavalry on parade at Fort Wallace, Kansas, from a photograph published as a woodcut in the July 27, 1867 issue of* Harper's Weekly. *The fort was the western-most post of the Smoky Hill defense system. Established in 1865, it was named after Brigadier General William H. Wallace, who was killed at the Battle of Shiloh. Situated at the junction of Pond Creek and the South Fork of the Smoky Hill River, it was the scene of many of the Seventh Cavalry's operations of 1867 and of Major George A. Forsyth's campaign of 1868 that led to the Battle of Beecher Island. Fort Wallace was abandoned in 1882. (Robert M. Utley, ed.,* Life in Custer's Cavalry, *286-87. Photograph courtesy Kansas State Historical Society.)*

61. *William Averill Comstock, known as "Medicine Bill," from an uncredited* carte de visite *that may be the work of Charles T. Smith of Topeka (it was found among a number of similar photographs bearing his imprint). Born on January 14, 1842, at Comstock, Michigan, Will Comstock was the son of General Horace H. Comstock, founder of the town, and Sarah Sabina Cooper, daughter of Judge Isaac Cooper of Cooperstown, New York, who was a brother of the novelist James Fenimore Cooper.*

His mother died in 1846 and his father in 1861. Will had a brother and three sisters. The brother died in infancy, and, following the deaths of their parents, he and the other children were placed in the care of relatives. By 1860, Will had gone west, where he settled at Cottonwood Springs, Nebraska Territory, and was listed in the census as an Indian trader with five hundred dollars' worth of property. Between 1860 and 1867 he achieved a great reputation on the frontier as a scout and interpreter, and in 1867 he was chief scout at Fort Wallace. He was Custer's favorite guide. Hickok, Cody, and the others had great respect for Comstock, and in later years Cody (or a

62. *No sharp copies of this photograph have come to light. This print, taken from an uncredited* carte de visite, *is believed to have been made circa 1867-68. Hickok appears to be wearing some kind of braided device attached to his coat lapels. (Courtesy Ethel Hickok)*

press agent) invented a spectacular shooting match between them, in which Cody supposedly won the title "Champion Buffalo Hunter of the World," but no evidence of such a contest exists.

Comstock was rarely in difficulties with his companions, but in January, 1868, he shot down an unarmed former companion who had swindled him. When charged with the murder before Justice M. E. Joyce at Hays, Kansas, he admitted the charge. The redoubtable judge reportedly replied, "You're a damned fool for admitting it; therefore I discharge you for lack of evidence."

Comstock was killed by Indians near Big Sandy Station in August, 1868, and his body was never recovered. (Ida Ipe, a descendant of Comstock, to the author, May 21, 1979. Photograph courtesy Kansas Collection, Kenneth Spencer Research Library, University of Kansas, Lawrence.)

63. *Fort Harker, Kansas, with the garrison on parade, from a photograph made by Alexander Gardner in September, 1867. (Courtesy Kansas State Historical Society.)*

64.   *This photograph, made by Alexander Gardner, was one of the large 13'' x 8½''
portfolio prints mounted on cards in his series "Across the Continent on the Union
Pacific Railway, E.D." Copies of the large prints are rare, but the stereoscopic versions
are more common. This photograph is titled (in pencil): "Group at Quarter Master's
Department, Fort Harker."*

    *Wild Bill is the figure at the extreme left in a large white hat. Two ivory-handled
Colt 1851 model Navy revolvers in open-topped holsters are worn butts forward on
his belt. Hickok's hat was the subject of an item in the Topeka State Record of
October 16, 1867, advising its readers that the hero of Harper's was in town: "You
will know him by his white hat and long hair. Get Harper and read the account of
his exploits, and then go and shake hands with Wild Bill."*

The military figure in the center is probably Colonel Henry Inman, who had recently assumed the position of quartermaster at the post. A close examination of an original print of this photograph shows that Hickok is slightly out of focus. His dress is similar to that worn in the Trott photograph, complete with bow tie, shown in Plates 91a and b.

Gardner reached Lawrence, Kansas, on September 21, 1867, and photographed its main street that morning. He was at Ellsworth on October 1, so it is possible that he photographed the scenes at Fort Harker on or about September 27. At the time this photograph was made, Hickok was not employed by the army but was a deputy U.S. marshal.

95

65. *The Sutler's store at Fort Harker, photographed by Alexander Gardner in September, 1867. Wild Bill was a frequent visitor to the Sutler's store. His favorite pastime in winter was to sit in a chair before its large stove, listening to and joining in the gossip. (Courtesy Kansas State Historical Society.)*

66. *Officers at Fort Harker, from a photograph by Alexander Gardner, September, 1867. The little girl features in other photographs made at the post, but the small, grinning boy at the far left makes only this one appearance. None of the group has been identified. (Courtesy Kansas State Historical Society.)*

67.   *The man at the upper left in this* carte de visite, *which bears Charles T. Smith's imprint, is believed to be Wild Bill, and the bearded figure at the right holding a pipe is H. C. Lindsay, a captain in the Eighteenth Kansas Regiment, which was formed for the duration of the Hancock Indian War. The remaining figures have not been identified. The regiment was mustered out in November, 1867—the approximate date of this photograph. The group is believed to be celebrating the end of the campaign.*

Lindsay served for a time as a deputy sheriff and for many years ran a livery stable. In later years he recalled many incidents in the life of Wild Bill, during both the territorial and the post-Civil War days. (Courtesy Kansas State Historical Society.)

68. *Colonel George A. Armes, from a woodcut copied from a photograph and published in his book* Ups and Downs of an Army Officer. *Armes served in the Tenth Cavalry and was noted for the number of times he was in difficulties with his superiors. Wild Bill first served as a guide to this colorful man in July, 1867, and was with him again in September, 1868. On September 2, Armes wrote in his journal that Wild Bill "came rushing in with fifteen of his scouts to inform me that a fresh Indian trail had been discovered." (Armes,* Ups and Downs, *273. Photograph courtesy Kansas State Historical Society.)*

69. *General Eugene A. Carr, in an engraving made from a photograph. Carr first fought Indians in the 1850s as a second lieutenant in the Regiment of Mounted Riflemen. During the Civil War he received the Medal of Honor for action at the Battle of Pea Ridge, and it was said of him that he would rather be a colonel of cavalry than the president of the United States.*

During the campaign against the Indians in 1868-69, he commanded the Fifth Cavalry. Buffalo Bill Cody was his chief of scouts, and he also met Hickok, who was attached to the Tenth Cavalry under the command of Brevet Brigadier General W. H. Penrose. Carr actively disliked Hickok, accusing him of failing to deliver dispatches to General Sheridan (official correspondence, however, refutes this) and later of losing the replies when an overcoat they were wrapped in was lost en route. Carr claimed that Hickok gambled with the officers and that most of them owed him money. He further stated that Hickok deliberately insulted Charles B. Autubees (Penrose's chief of scouts), and his eldest son Mariano—who were of mixed Indian and Mexican descent—by calling them "mongrels." They were afraid of him. When Carr said he intended to get rid of Wild Bill, it was the Autubees, curiously, who pleaded that he be allowed to stay. Carr also reported that Hickok informed him that General Sheridan had told him to keep an eye on the so-called colored troops and, if he had any trouble, to come to him.

Carr's allegations, some of them made during the 1860s and others in his old age, require an evaluation outside the scope of the present study, but they are nonetheless an interesting insight into his relationship with Hickok. (Gen. E. A. Carr, "Carr's Campaign of 1868-69," manuscript in the possession of James T. King, to whom I am indebted for a copy. Photograph courtesy Kansas State Historical Society.)

CHAPTER FOUR

Peace Officer and Pistoleer
(1869-1871)

Wild Bill spent the latter part of March and much of April, 1869, at his mother's home at Troy Grove. His sister Lydia recalled that the family knew little of his wound until it became infected. A doctor was called, who lanced it, drawing the flesh back to scrape the bone. Her brother refused chloroform, and when she grew faint, he grasped the lamp she was holding and held it until the operation was finished, "never flinching once."[1]

Hickok, however, soon missed the plains and at the first opportunity returned west. Early in May he was ordered to Fort Wallace in his capacity as a deputy U.S. marshal to arrest two men accused of stealing mules. Together with two witnesses he and his prisoners took the train for Topeka, where both men eventually went on trial.[2]

In Topeka, Hickok learned that U.S. Marshal Charles C. Whiting was in trouble with the government. A number of Pawnee Indians had been killed at Ellsworth, and several of Whiting's deputies were allegedly involved. Whiting's commission was revoked, and in his place Dana W. Houston was appointed marshal. Houston promptly interviewed all of Whiting's deputies at Leavenworth and dismissed many of them. Wild Bill, however, was one of those he retained, and Hickok continued to work in the Hays City area.[3]

Hays City was founded in September, 1867, and rapidly earned a reputation for lawlessness. Attempts to establish law and order were not a great success. By the summer of 1869 the town was without an efficient police force, and Ellis County had no sheriff. A petition to the governor in July, requesting that he appoint one R. A. Eccles as sheriff, was ignored. Early in August the county commissioners, aided by the vigilance committee, held an election in which Wild Bill was chosen as acting sheriff. The commissioners made this move to combat the city's growing lawlessness because existing statute books provided for it, but the governor disagreed with their interpretation of the statutes and declared Hickok's appointment illegal. Nonetheless, the citizens of Hays welcomed Wild Bill, as did the press.[4]

On August 22, Wild Bill shot a man named Bill Melvin (or Mulvey), described as an "intoxicated rough" and a "wolf," who was shooting up the town in company with a number of equally inebriated companions. Melvin died soon afterward.[5]

Within weeks Hickok's status as the law in Hays City was unquestioned by most of the inhabitants, and it was late in September before he again faced serious trouble. On September 27 he was called upon to break up a near-riot in John Bitter's Beer Saloon, and during the affray he shot and killed Sam Strawhun. Despite some contradictory evidence, a coroner's jury returned a verdict that Strawhun "came to his death from a pistol wound at the hands of J. B. Hickok, and that the shooting of said Stringham [*sic*] was justifiable."[6] Early residents recalled that Hickok meandered along the streets armed with his two favorite pistols, a pair of Colt 1851 Navy revolvers, and that he was not averse to displaying his marksmanship when the mood possessed him.[7]

When a man named Bob Connors murdered a drover named Hammy at Pond Creek, he fled to Hays, where he was arrested and placed in the Fort Hays guardhouse. Hickok, accompanied by his deputy Peter ("Rattlesnake Pete") Lanahan, appeared before the post commander and presented a warrant issued by John Whiteford, justice of the peace at Pond City, requesting that Connors be handed over to Sheriff Hickok. Because Wild Bill held no commission, the warrant's request was refused. Following a protracted correspondence between the governor and the post commander, Connors was eventually removed to Sheridan for trial. After an examination of his case, however, he was acquitted and released.[8]

Two men employed by the post quartermaster at Fort Hays fell out when one of them caught the other unscrewing nuts from his wagon. The pair shot it out, and one man was badly wounded. The other ran into a saloon, and, although Hickok prevented him from being lynched, an irate citizen managed to shoot and wound him. Both men ended up in the hospital together and, following recovery, became the best of friends.[9]

The November election was expected to end in a riot, and the post commander of Fort Hays was prepared to take military action in that event. It passed off very quietly, however, with the result that J. B. Hickok, Independant, polled 89 votes and his deputy, Peter Lanihan, Democrat, 114.

Hickok remained in office for two months, until about December 31, during which time he was again very active as a deputy U.S. marshal.[10] During this period he was mostly concerned with the apprehension of illegal timber cutters, and he made several arrests and brought the men before U.S. Commissioners Hill P. Wilson and Lewis Hauback to swear out complaints or to receive warrants authorizing him to make such arrests. That he occasionally delivered prisoners to Topeka was noted by the press. On December 9 the Topeka *Daily Commonwealth* surpassed itself and poetically remarked about Wild Bill, "Long may he be at Hays, 'Shake his ambrosial locks and give the nod, the Stamp of fate, the sanction of a god!'"

Late in December, Private William Gleason of Company I, Third Infantry, was lodged in the Fort Hays guardhouse charged with murder. The post commander requested that Gleason be removed for trial by the civil authorities and said that he would hold him until Hickok arrived. Hickok, however, was in Topeka at the time, so the colonel arranged a military escort instead.[11]

On January 2, 1870, Wild Bill's old friend, former U.S. Marshal Whiting, died after a long illness. Later in the month, on January 20, Hickok arrested a man named Isaac Shindle, who was charged with the illegal manufacture of cigars.[12] During the next two months Hickok spent much of his time at Junction City, making occasional visits to Topeka, where in February he was involved in a fistfight on the corner of Sixth Street and Kansas Avenue. A man apparently insulted him, and Hickok promptly knocked him down. Wild Bill was arrested and "fined five dollars for striking straight out from the shoulder and consequently hitting a man."[13]

March found Hickok at Jefferson City, Missouri, where he was the guest of the legislature. The press noted that he had many friends among the members. By late April, however, he was back in Topeka, where he was issued a subpoena and ordered to Junction City to serve it on John Schooler and John Tucker, summoning them to testify in the case of the *U.S. v. Manley B. Gilman and James Stitt*, who had been indicted for larceny and the misappropriation of United States property (a number of horses and mules).[14]

Unconfirmed reports assert that Hickok visited Texas in June, 1870, and appeared in Colonel Ginger's Circus at Sherman, but by July he was back in Kansas. On the evening of July 17 he was in a saloon in Hays City, drinking and talking to the bartender, when he was attacked by a number of drunken Seventh Cavalry troopers from Fort Hays. Hickok was pulled to the ground, and one man thrust a pistol barrel into his ear and pulled the trigger. The cap failed to explode, however, and by that time Hickok had one of his own pistols out and working. He shot one man through the wrist and knee and the other through the body. When their companions also turned on him,

Hickok was forced to make a hasty exit. Private Jerry Lonergan, the man shot through the knee, soon recovered and was returned to duty, but his companion, Private John Kile, died in the Fort Hays hospital the following day.[15]

Public reaction to the shooting was mixed. Those who knew the facts were generally in agreement that the demon drink had been largely responsible for the incident and that Hickok's action had been in self-defense. Others, however, thought that he should be summarily dealt with. The military, accustomed to such incidents, took no action, except to state in their report that Kile died from a pistol wound received in a drunken row and not in the line of duty.[16]

Hickok's movements after that fight caused much speculation. Some thought he was wounded and had perhaps died, while others were convinced he was hiding out. It now seems clear that he was neither wounded nor in hiding. He returned to Junction City and again became a familiar figure on the streets. On August 15 a man named John McAllister passed a counterfeit twenty-dollar note at Abilene, which had been traced back to him. Deputy U.S. Marshal Hickok was alerted, and on September 15 a warrant was issued on his complaint, and he was ordered to Abilene to arrest McAllister. It is possible that he enlisted the aid of Abilene's marshal, Thomas James Smith, in seeking out his man. If that is so, then Hickok probably was known both to the citizens of Abilene and also to Smith whose death would soon result in Hickok's own appointment as Abilene's marshal.[17]

Abilene was a sleepy village, a stagecoach stop, and later a lonely halt on the tracks of the Union Pacific Railway, Eastern Division (renamed the Kansas Pacific Railway in 1869), when it was "discovered" by Joseph G. McCoy, a cattle buyer from Illinois who was eager to find a point from which he could ship Texas cattle to the East without infringing upon the Kansas quarantine laws.

After the Civil War, many thousands of longhorn cattle were running wild in the brush country of Texas. Rounding them up was simple; finding a means and a route to eastern markets was not. McCoy's discovery of Abilene came after a long search and hours of wrangling with various railroad officials about providing shipping facilities. Finally he persuaded the Union Pacific to put in a one-hundred-car switch at Abilene. Shipping pens were constructed there, as well as the now legendary three-story Drover's Cottage hotel. On September 5, 1867, the first trainload of cattle was shipped to Chicago, and Abilene was in business.[18]

There were many cattle routes up from Texas, but by far the most famous was the Chisholm Trail. Named for Jesse Chisholm, a half-blood trader, it wound up from the Río Grande and through Indian Territory as far as Wichita, where it officially ended. From there on it was known as McCoy's Extension, or the Abilene Trail.[19]

With the herds came that strange, now part-mythical breed of men history recalls as cowboys, whose ability to control the half-wild and totally unpredictable Texas longhorns is legendary. Credited with a superior skill as rider, roper, and six-shooter virtuoso, the cowboy remains unsurpassed—except, perhaps, by the gunfighter, with whom he is often confused—as the most potent figure in American folklore. His riding and roping skills, and his bravery when confronted by stampedes and other dangers on the trail, are unquestionable. As a "pistoleer," however, the cowboy could rarely hit a barn door from the inside. When he was drunk, and letting off steam in a cowtown, he was potentially more dangerous than the cattle.

To combat the Texans and to control the gamblers and prostitutes who descended upon the cattle towns like locusts, town councils passed ordinances against gambling, prostitution, and the carrying and discharging of firearms in the street. To enforce the law required a strong police force, and Abilene's lead in this matter was followed by Ellsworth, Wichita, Dodge City, and other towns that eventually took on the profits and perils associated with the cattle trade.

By 1869 law and order was badly needed in Abilene, and what law there was in the surrounding townships was insufficient. Abilene demanded a police force of its own. In September a number of citizens presented a petition before the probate judge of Dickinson County, requesting incorporation as a city. The judge granted the request, and Abilene became a third-class city with power to elect a mayor, a council, and a police force. Theodore C. Henry was selected as acting mayor, pending a proper election, and a number of ordinances were passed relative to gambling and prostitution. But the most urgent need was for a marshal.

Thomas J. Smith was appointed to the post by Mayor Henry on June 4, 1870. He proved very effective, but on November 2, while making an arrest on behalf of the county sheriff—who was too ill to do it himself—Smith was murdered. Patrick Hand, a gunsmith, became the next marshal, and he was replaced by Smith's erstwhile deputy, James H. McDonald. The 1871 cattle season, however, was destined to be the biggest in the town's history, and the city needed a strong man to maintain order. Historians do not agree on the circumstances under which he was offered the job, but on April 15, 1871, Wild Bill became the marshal of Abilene.[20]

During the eight months he held the post, Hickok had a succession of deputies, some good and some bad, but it was agreed by most people that during his reign violence was contained in the area known as "McCoy's Addition" (where the prostitutes carried on their trade) and in Texas Street, where saloons and gambling dens proliferated. The tracks of the Kansas Pacific Railway separated these places from the "respectable" part of town.

On the night of October 5, Hickok was involved in a fight with a number of drunken Texans outside the Alamo Saloon. He and their leader, gambler Philip Coe, shot it out at a distance of about eight feet. Coe's shots passed through Hickok's coat and between his legs, but Wild Bill's bullets lodged in Coe's stomach. A man rushed between both men, brandishing a pistol, and Hickok shot him. It was later discovered that the second victim was Michael Williams, a Kansas City bartender and a special policeman hired by the Novelty Theatre to keep the amorous Texans away from the showgirls. Hearing the shots, he forgot Hickok's earlier warning to keep out of the way. He was unrecognized as he rushed out of the darkness and into the glare of the streetlights and was mistaken by Hickok for an enemy. Williams died instantly.[21]

Coe was helped to a nearby house, where he died in great agony three days later. Once Hickok realized what had happened to Williams, he was reported to have gone through the streets and saloons chasing out the Texans or disarming those who wished to remain. But within days he was a marked man, and the Texans offered a large reward to anyone who killed him. Friends reported that he began carrying a sawed-off shotgun as he patrolled the streets. On a trip to Topeka late in November his life was threatened, but he was warned by a fellow traveler and was able to confront his would-be assassins. Drawing his pistols, he forced them to remain on the train as it pulled out.[22]

By early December the cattle trade had ended. The citizens, fearful of what the next season might bring—and under pressure from the farming community to get rid of the trade—finally decided to ban it. On December 13, Hickok was dismissed because the city no longer needed his services. In February, 1872, Abilene published a notice urging the Texans to take their cattle elsewhere because the citizens could no longer submit to the evils of the trade. By then Wild Bill had also gone, leaving behind him a reputation that, with time, became an important part of his legend.

Haus City -1868- South Main St.
Burned out in 1881.

70. *South Main Street, Hays City, 1868. Most of the buildings shown here were destroyed by a fire in 1881. Hays was founded in September, 1867, and for a short period was the end of the track for the Union Pacific Railway, Eastern Division. On December 5, 1867, Thomas Gannon was elected the first sheriff of Ellis County, and William L. Totten and Peter Carrol, were made constables of Big Creek Township. Gannon made his headquarters in Hays and established there the rudiments of law and order. By April, 1868, however, he had disappeared, presumably murdered from ambush. A succession of policemen followed, including two sheriffs, before the county commissioners (aided by a vigilance committee) elected Wild Bill to serve as acting sheriff from August, 1869, until the November elections. Although the governor declared Hickok's election illegal, the commissioners evidently had followed existing statutes, and their decision was welcomed by local residents. (Rosa,* Wild Bill, *140; Rev. Blaine Burkey,* Wild Bill Hickok, *5-6. Photograph courtesy Kansas State Historical Society.)*

71. *Wild Bill was appointed a deputy U.S. marshal in 1867 by then U.S. Marshal Charles C. Whiting. This letter was written following a request from Whiting to the post commander of Fort Hays to advise Wild Bill in the event that he had any civilian prisoners accused of federal offenses. A sergeant and five privates were detailed to accompany Hickok (assisted by Buffalo Bill) in transporting eleven prisoners to Topeka for trial. The alleged leader of the gang, Captain James Smith, formerly of the Seventh Kansas Regiment, was arrested soon afterward, brought to Topeka "in irons," and*

Hays City, Kansas
March 28th 18[68]

Capt Sam Crawshine
Comdg Post of Fort Hays Kans

Capt:

I have the honor
to request that a guard of a Corpl and
five men may be detailed to assist me in
conveying the prisoners of the U.S. Marshal
now in the Post Guard House to Topeka Kans
I would respectfully call your attention
to the number and character of these prisoners
and the feeling in their behalf in this Community which renders a guard of U.S. Soldiers
absolutely necessary.

I am Captain, very respectfully
Your obd't Servt
J B Hickok
Deft. U.S. Marshal

placed on trial. He was found not guilty and released. Some of the other prisoners are believed to be escapees who, assisted by outsiders, had made a break from the new jail. (Fort Hays Letter File, Letters Received, KSHS; Topeka Weekly Leader, April 2 and 8, 1868; Topeka State Record, May 27, 1868; Case no. 619, U.S. v. James Smith: Stealing Government Property, Record Group 21, Federal Archives, Kansas City, Mo. Photograph courtesy National Archives, Washington, D.C.)

72. *Samuel O. Strawhun, from a family tintype. Strawhun was one of the few victims of Wild Bill's pistol prowess whose photograph has survived. Born in southern Missouri on October 10, 1845, Sam spent his early years in Illinois and by the late 1860s was employed by the United States Army, first as a teamster and later as a courier. He worked briefly for the county court and then spent a short time incarcerated in the Fort Hays guardhouse on a federal warrant (the contents of which have not been disclosed). He was a signatory on the petition circulated in the summer of 1869 supporting R. A. Eccles for sheriff of Ellis County, Kansas.*

Some weeks later Strawhun and Joseph Weiss, a late inmate of the state penitentiary and a former deputy U.S. marshal, were ordered out of town. The pair made the mistake of attacking one of the vigilantes, A. B. Webster, the Hays Post Office clerk. They pulled their pistols on him, but Webster was quicker and shot Weiss, who died soon afterward. Strawhun escaped.

On the night of September 27, 1869, Sam turned up again with a number of cronies and decided to "clear out" John Bitter's Beer Saloon. Hickok was sent for, and when he insisted that Strawhun return some empty beer glasses to the bar and Strawhun in return threatened his life, Hickok shot him through the head, killing him instantly. The Leavenworth Daily Commercial *reported on October 5: "Too much credit cannot be given to Wild Bill for his endeavour to rid this town of such dangerous characters as this Stranhan [sic] was." (Junction City* Weekly Union, *July 31, 1869;* Rosa, Wild Bill, *146-48. Photograph courtesy Mrs. Jean Fisherkeller.)*

WILD BILL—From a Photograph.

a

73a–d *(pages 111-113). The engraving of "Wild Bill—From a Photograph" (73a), published in W. E. Webb's* Buffalo Land *in 1872, was one of many woodcuts prepared from photographs by the Bureau of Illustration at Rochester, New York. The only copy of the original photograph known to me is reproduced as Plate 73b. Discovered in 1955, it is a carte de visite mounted on a plain card with rounded edges and has no*

b

c

photographer's imprint. The original plate was made between 1868 and 1870, and the moustache and goatee sported by Hickok are also featured in a celebrated cartoon published in 1871 and reproduced as Plate 88.

Webb, an agent for the Union Pacific Railway, Eastern Division, purchased from the railroad the land on which Hays City was built. His Big Creek Land Company sold lots in the infant city, and he became friendly with Hickok, Cody, and many other early residents. A great admirer of Hickok, Webb urged him to abandon the frontier and take up a less warlike occupation. Hickok agreed that clerking in a store might be safer but said it was not the life for him.

The photographer of Plate 73b is unknown, but A. P. Trott has been suggested as possibly the man who made it. Plate 73c poses similar problems; it, too, is uncredited, but in 1908 a retouched version was "copyrighted" by one Perkins and is currently on sale as a colored postcard. The version reproduced here is the best-known copy and came from the collection of Chauncey Thomas, a noted western writer and gun enthusiast during the 1920s and 1930s.

d

*The photograph shown as Plate 73d has rarely been reproduced, but it is believed
to be from the same period as the others. In it Hickok is dressed in the jacket seen
in the other photographs, but here he is wearing the crossed-striped trousers shown
only in Plate 73c. This photograph was discovered in the collection of the late Joseph
E. Stimson. Stimson practiced photography in Cheyenne from 1889 (when he was
nineteen years old) until his death in 1952. He left a stock of over eight thousand
negatives. Some of his plates were the work of others, and the Wild Bill portrait is
an old print, presumably acquired during his long years in business. Like the others
included here, it bears no imprint. (Mrs. Paula West, Photographic Section, Wyoming
State Archives and Historical Department, to the author, October 26, 1976. Plates 73a
and b courtesy Kansas State Historical Society; Plate 73c courtesy Colorado State
Historical Society, Denver; Plate 73d courtesy Wyoming State Archives, Cheyenne.)*

74. *Hill P. Wilson. In 1869, Wilson was a United States commissioner at Fort Hays and dealt with a number of prisoners brought before him by Deputy U.S. Marshal Hickok. He later was in partnership with his brothers as sutlers at Fort Hays, and eventually became a successful merchant banker. In his old age he delighted in recalling various events in Hickok's colorful career at Hays. (Courtesy Kansas State Historical Society.)*

75. *The famous Otero and Sellar store at Hays. Miguel Otero, the son of one of the partners, recalled in later years a childhood admiration for Wild Bill and a dislike of Buffalo Bill Cody. Whereas Wild Bill was "always kind and considerate toward others" and a "real joy to meet," Buffalo Bill was "rather selfish and wanted all the pomp and grandeur for himself." Hickok, he believed, was "genuinely brave: I never met his equal for courage on the frontier," but he said of Cody that he "would not call him a brave man; he was much too cautious. He was smart enough to arrange matters so he would always be in the clear." Nonetheless, Otero did concede that Cody was a commanding figure and had a good brain for business—an essential asset in the world of show business. (Miguel Otero,* My Life on the Frontier, *1:14, 32-35. Photograph courtesy Kansas State Historical Society.)*

76. *James M. Harvey, governor of Kansas in 1869, when Hickok attempted to remove Bob Connors from the Fort Hays guardhouse. The governor disagreed with the Ellis County commissioners about the legality of the statutes under which Hickok was elected sheriff. In January, 1870, to prevent any similar misunderstandings, Governor Harvey recommended to the state legislature that the statutes be changed to allow the governor to appoint a sheriff, in the event of a vacancy, until a proper election could be held. (Junction City* Union, *January 8, 1870. Photograph courtesy Kansas State Historical Society.)*

77a–d *(pages 117-119).   Records of Hickok's service as a policeman in Hays City are scarce, and the only evidence to come to light is shown as Plate 77a. Believed to have been presented by Wild Bill to Ellis County in 1869, it was discovered in the late 1870s and donated to the Kansas State Historical Society in 1882 by J. H. Downing of Hays City. For many years it was accepted as a rare example of Hickok's handwriting and signature. A comparison of this document and authenticated Hickok signatures (77b and c) reveals that it was written on his behalf.*

It is curious that photographs have appeared in recent years bearing alleged Hickok signatures that, on examination, have proved to be forgeries. Perhaps the most notorious is the one bearing the inscription, "Sincerely J. B. Hickok." A comparison of this signature and the J. B. Hickok on the second line of the Ellis

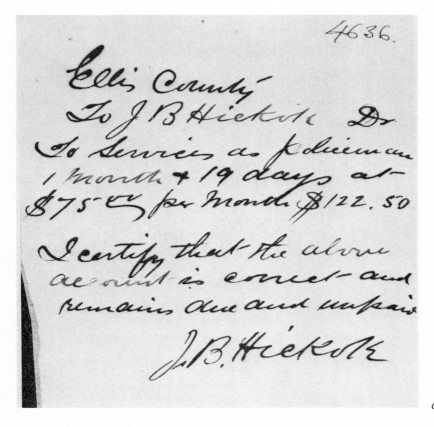

4636.

Ellis County
To J B Hickok Dr
To Services as policeman
1 month & 19 days at
$75.00 per month $122.50

I certify that the above
account is correct and
remains due and unpaid

J.B. Hickok

a

County document shows them to be identical, and the conclusion must be that it is a copy. Unfortunately, the original photograph has never been submitted to expert analysis, so the age of the inscription is unknown.

The document reproduced as Plate 77d is interesting because it concerns John Hobbs—a character long associated with the Hickok legend. Until recently the story of Hickok arresting Hobbs and some of his associates (for stealing timber from government lands) has defied verification. Papers and court records relative to Ellis County, discovered in the Federal Archives and Record Center at Kansas City, Missouri, however, disclosed a case against Hobbs and others. Following a preliminary hearing before Hill P. Wilson, Hobbs and his companions were taken to Topeka for trial, but no record of a trial has been found. Contemporary sources suggest that the defendants were discharged for want of evidence and that Hobbs later ran a drugstore in Hays City. (United States v. Charles Hamilton and others: *Preliminary Hearing, Record Group 21, Federal Archives, Kansas City, Mo.; Hays City* Republican, April 10, 1897. Plate 77a courtesy Kansas State Historical Society; Plates 77b-d courtesy Federal Archives and Record Center, Kansas City, Mo.)

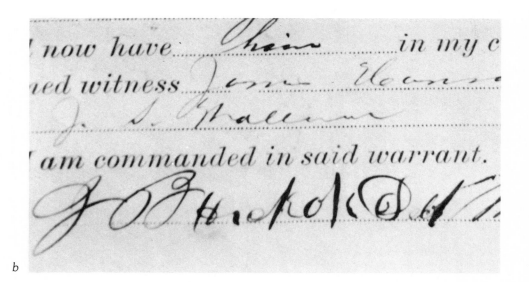

now have _____ _____ in my c

ed witness _____ _____

_____ _____

am commanded in said warrant.

b

The UNITED STATES, U.S. Marshal

186 _____ To J. B. Hickok Dr.

To service as Deputy U.S. Marshal
from January 1st 1865 to June 30
1866 inclusive

615 00

Received payment of C. C. Whiting U.S. Marshal
District of Kansas.
(Signed in Duplicate.)

J. B. Hickok

c

The United States of America,

To the Marshal of the District of Kansas, Greeting:

Whereas, Complaint upon oath has this day been made before me by
J. B. Hickok
charging and alleging that _Chas. Hamilton, Chas. Vernon & John Hobbs_
late of _Hays City_ in said District, heretofore,
to wit: on the _Tenth_ day of _____ A. D. 18__
at _District of Kansas_ aforesaid
_unlawfully did cut and cause to be removed certain timber growing
upon the lands of the United States to wit: One hundred oak trees of the value
of One hundred dollars, One hundred cottonwood trees of the value of one hundred
dollars and one hundred oak trees of the value of one hundred fifty
dollars with intent then and there to dispose of and use the same for
the use of the army of the United States_
contrary to the act of Congress in such case provided, which complaint is hereon indorsed.

You are Therefore Hereby Commanded, that you take the said _Chas. Hamilton,
Chas. Vernon, John Hobbs_ if he shall be found in your District, and _them_
safely keep so that you may bring _them_
before me, a Commissioner appointed by the Circuit Court of the United States
for the District of Kansas, under and by virtue of the several acts of Congress
in such case made and provided, at my office at _Hays, Kan._
in said District to be dealt with according to law.

You are also Further Commanded, in the name of the President of the United States,
to summon _J. D. Hamilton of Junction City_
_1st & 2nd N. C__k 3 N. Sofo_
to appear before me, said Commissioner, where you shall have the said
_____ to testify _their_ knowledge on
behalf of the United States, touching the matter of said complaint, and have
you then and there this warrant. Hereof fail not.

Witness my Hand and Seal, This _16th_ day of _December_
in the year of our Lord one thousand eight hundred and _Sixty Nine_

W. F. Wilson
United States Commissioner for the District of Kansas.

District of Kansas, ss.

I hereby certify and return that on the _16_ day of _December_
A. D. 186_9_ by virtue of the above warrant, I did arrest the above named
Chas. Hamilton, Chas. Vernon & John Hobbs
and now have _them_ in my custody, and that I did summon the above
named witness _____

as I am commanded in said warrant.
J. B. Hickok Dep. Marshal.
~~Deputy~~ Marshal.

By _____ ~~Deputy Marshal.~~

d

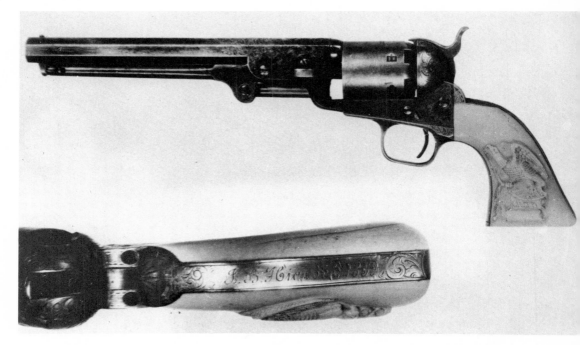

78a, b. *This factory-engraved Colt 1851 Navy revolver, serial number 138813, is said to be one of a pair presented to Hickok at Hays City in 1869. Some sources claim that they were the gift of Senator Henry Wilson in grateful appreciation of a guided tour of the plains; others assert that the pistols were presented to Hickok by the Union Pacific Railway, Eastern Division, for "cleaning up Hays City." The Wilson tour never took place, and no verification of the railroad story has been found.*

The photograph has been published a number of times since the early 1950s, and until quite recently it was thought to have been made by the Colt Company in the 1920s, when the pistol was sent to them for identification. The original photograph, however, bears the name of a Los Angeles photographer, and it clearly shows that the backstrap inscription read: "J. B. Hickock, 1869." Shown at 78b, however, is a recent photograph of the backstrap, and it can be seen that the second "c" in Hickok's name has been removed by an expert engraver. At this writing it is not known who this was or when it was done. The present owner, who wishes to remain anonymous, has assured me that any alteration must have been made before his wife's father obtained the pistol in 1932. The last time the pistol was on public view was in 1936-37, when it was exhibited in Chicago as part of the publicity for Gary Cooper's film The Plainsman. *It was then locked in a bank vault, where it remained until the early 1970s.*

Unfortunately, the history of this revolver is not well documented. Until 1932 it

was in the collection of M. C. Clark, a well-known gun collector of the time, and he claimed that his father received the pistol as a gift from J. X. Beidler, a former vigilante who was a "United States marshal" at Deadwood, Dakota Territory, in 1876. Beidler officiated at Hickok's funeral and kept his pistol. This story is nonsense, of course, and a search of available records at the Colt factory at Hartford, Connecticut, has failed to find any reference to the weapon. But this is not surprising: in 1864 most of the factory was destroyed in a fire, and very few records from the percussion era survived. Nonetheless, it is possible to date the pistol to about 1864, which means it had been in a dealer's stock for about five years before it was purchased for presentation—assuming, of course, that it is genuine.

The suggestion that the pistol was one of the pair depicted in several photographs of Hickok cannot be correct. The Date "1869" precludes the Fort Harker photograph of 1867, and the famous buckskin photograph has so far defied accurate dating.

Time may provide more answers to the riddle of this revolver; apart from doubts about its link with Hickok, there is the matter of the changed inscription. That alone has seriously depleted its value, both as a collector's piece and as a frontier relic. (R. L. Wilson to the author, 1975-77 correspondence. Plate 78a courtesy the Connecticut State Library, Hartford; Plate 78b from a private collection.)

79. *This revolver is a licensed Belgian copy, made in Liege, of the British 1855 model Beaumont Adams revolver. It is a five-shot double-action weapon, .54-bore (about .45-caliber), and it was retailed by Deane, Adams and Deane, 30, King William Street, London. On the side of the frame, immediately behind the cylinder, can be seen the remains of a sliding safety catch designed to fit into a slot cut into the rear of the cylinder.*

Until 1855 most English revolvers were self-cockers (that is, the trigger was pulled to cock and release the hammer), but in February of that year Lieutenant F. E. Beaumont of the Royal Engineers patented an improvement to the existing lockwork of the Adams revolver that enabled the weapon to be cocked and fired either by the trigger or by a thumb-cocked hammer (like Colt single-action revolvers). This was the first true "double-action" system, and it proved to be immensely popular.

Out west, however, the double-action revolver was never very popular with gunfighters, and cowboys detested them. Several writers have alleged that at one point in his career Hickok carried a pair of double-action revolvers, presumably of the type illustrated (he died before Colt produced their first double-action revolvers). Mrs. Frank Wilstach, widow of the author of a book on Hickok, presented this pistol to the Kansas State Historical Society in 1934, claiming that her husband had obtained it on the understanding that Hickok once owned it, but she offered no documentation. (Courtesy Kansas State Historical Society.)

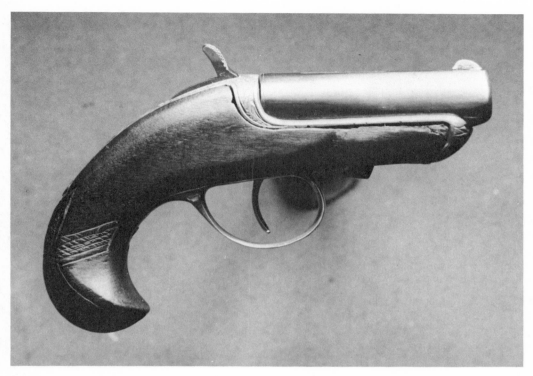

80. *According to several writers, Hickok armed himself with a pair of Williamson dual-ignition derringers. These .41-caliber weapons were first manufactured in 1866, and they were popular with gamblers and others who relied upon the small "hide-out" pistols when larger weapons would have been difficult to get at. Releasing a catch beneath the barrel enables it to slide forward. A .41-caliber rimfire cartridge can be loaded or a metal tube—complete with a percussion nipple—inserted, enabling the shooter to load the weapon with loose powder and ball and a percussion cap.*

81. *Joseph Geiting McCoy, about 1871 when mayor of Abilene. Born on a farm near Spring Creek, Sangamon County, Illinois, on December 21, 1837, McCoy grew up among cattle and cattlemen and was an expert in various methods of cattle shipment. The end of the Civil War and the need for Southern trade and expansion, coupled with a demand for meat in the East and the Far West, spurred him to reestablish such a business.*

Early in 1867, McCoy went to Kansas, representing the family firm of William K. McCoy and Brothers, and tried to find a suitable route across the state to a railroad. Quarantine laws and the fear of Texas (or Spanish) Fever, which killed domestic stock but had no effect on the Texas longhorns, led to bitterness among settlers and farmers. Early droves were met with resistance, and the drovers and cowboys were attacked.

Among the early routes chosen by McCoy was one to Baxter Springs, but it lacked a rail link. Following months of frustration, McCoy finally persuaded the Union Pacific Railway, Eastern Division, to put in a one-hundred-car switch at Abilene. Within months, shipping pens and other buildings had been erected, and Abilene became a cattle town.

Following the murder of Policeman Tom Smith and the election of the first official town council, the need for a marshal was paramount. In later years, when recalling his choice of Hickok as Abilene's marshal, McCoy declared: "Wild Bill was the squarest man I ever saw. He broke up all unfair gambling, made professional gamblers move their tables into the light, and when they became drunk stopped the game." He reportedly declared that Hickok had killed forty-three men before his arrival in Abilene, but perhaps he was misquoted.

McCoy's contract with the Union Pacific, Eastern Division, had not been a written one, but they had agreed to pay him as much as five dollars a carload for all cattle shipped over their line. So confident was he of payment that in 1870 he bought out his brothers, promising to pay them as soon as he received his money from the railroad. The company failed to pay, and McCoy brought suit against the Union Pacific's successor, the Kansas Pacific Railway. In July, 1871, the Kansas Supreme Court

82. *Theodore C. Henry, from a photograph made sometime after his days in Abilene. Henry had been an unsuccessful cotton grower and an unwilling law student before he found his destiny in Abilene. He was persuaded to settle there by McCoy, who, despite their differences in local politics, remained Henry's lifelong friend. "T. C." (as he was called by most people) realized that the future of Kansas lay not in cattle but farming. He conducted well-guarded experiments that resulted in a strain of wheat that established his reputation and earned him the title "Wheat King of Kansas."*

Although in later years he had little to say about Wild Bill and the cattle days — apart from his speech at the dedication of the memorial to Tom Smith—his two younger brothers, Stuart and Samuel, devoted much of their time recording Hickok's exploits. Following a distinguished career that included banking and a professional interest in irrigation (he even earned the title "Irrigation King of Colorado"), Henry died in Denver in 1914, greatly mourned. (Stuart Henry, Conquering Our Great American Plains, viii-xii; Stewart P. Verckler, Cowtown Abilene, 14-16, 45, 56. Photograph courtesy Kansas State Historical Society.)

ruled in his favor, but by then it was too late: McCoy was broke. He never again achieved the success he had enjoyed in Abilene.

When the Tom Smith monument was dedicated in August, 1904, McCoy, who had been invited to speak, was unable to attend the ceremony because a flash flood had washed out the railroad line from Wichita. Had McCoy been present, perhaps Hickok, too, would have had a hearing that day. McCoy died in Kansas City, Missouri, in 1915 and was buried in Wichita. (Wayne Gard, The Chisholm Trail, 59, 253n.; Topeka Capital, August 30, 1908. Photograph courtesy the late Stewart P. Verckler.)

83a, b.   *Plate 83a is alleged to be Thomas James Smith, marshal of Abilene in 1870. The photograph came to light in the late 1890s among a number of relics of the cattle days. Described as a daguerreotype it was copied by the Abilene photographer Forney, and the money raised from sales of prints to old settlers was almost enough by itself to pay for Smith's monument.*

Despite intensive research by many people, Tom Smith remains a mystery man. The Abilene census of 1870 gave his age as forty and his birthplace as New York. Reports that he had served as a New York policeman cannot be verified. Some have claimed that he was the notorious "Bear River" Tom Smith, a troubleshooter for the Union Pacific Railway who led a riot at Bear River, or Bear Town, Wyoming Territory, in November, 1868. According to the Deseret News *of December 24, 1868, Tom Smith was sent to the Utah State Penitentiary, but no proof of this has been found. In any event, if it was the same man, his sentence was short.*

Tom Smith proved a good officer and his original monthly salary of $150 was later raised to $225 — the highest sum Abilene ever paid during its period as a cowtown. Mounted upon his huge horse Silverheels, he patrolled the city regularly, and, although he carried a fine pair of ornate Colt pistols he rarely drew them. The more violent of the Texas cowboys — who expected to be challenged by weapons and not fists — were baffled by Smith, who boldly approached his pistol-wielding adversaries and, once within range of them, wasted no time knocking them down.

Smith's reign came to a tragic end on November 2, 1870, when he and James McDonald, his deputy, went to arrest a settler named Andrew McConnell, who had

been charged with murdering a man named John Shea. McConnell produced a rifle, and Smith, in trying to wrest it from him, was shot in the chest. At that moment Moses Miles, McConnell's neighbor, joined in, first hitting Smith over the head with a gun and then all but decapitating him with an ax. McDonald had rushed to Smith's assistance and exchanged shots with the pair, shooting off two of Miles's fingers, but McConnell and Miles escaped. Eventually captured and put on trial, Miles and McConnell were sentenced in March, 1871, to long terms in the state penitentiary (most Abilene residents would have preferred the rope).

   McDonald's reputation, despite his efforts and his subsequent pursuit of the murderers, was badly tarnished by the episode. He proved his ability as the marshal of Newton during the following year, but he is still remembered in Abilene as the man who deserted Tom Smith.

   Shown at 83b is a copy of a tintype owned by the family of L. S. Sargent, an early resident of Junction City. It is purportedly a photograph of the young Sargent and Wild Bill made about 1870, when Hickok frequented the Sargent drugstore. It is obviously not Hickok, but it could well be Thomas James Smith, elegantly dressed in a manner quite out of keeping with the normal attire of a cowtown policeman. (Kansas City Star, May 30, 1904; Minute Book of the City Council of Abilene, 29, 34, Manuscripts Division, KSHS; Junction City Union, November 5, 1871. Plate 83a courtesy Kansas State Historical Society; Plate 83b courtesy the George Smith Public Library, Junction City, Kansas.

84.   *Abilene, from a photograph made in the 1870s, looking north from the railroad tracks. The courthouse is in the center, and T. C. Henry's office is at left. Abilene was laid out in a pattern typical of many Western towns.*

Running east-west and parallel to the railroad was Texas Street (later renamed South First Street). At its main intersection was Cedar Street, which ran south from the railroad some five blocks east of Mud Creek. East from Cedar Street was a small street known simply as "A," at the end of which was Joseph G. McCoy's famous Drover's Cottage and the Shane and Henry real estate office. A collection of shacks north of the railroad housed the dance halls and brothels. (Courtesy Kansas State Historical Society.)

128

85.   *A small part of Abilene's Great Western Stockyard, looking south from Gordon's grain elevator. The cattle were herded into the pens and then eased into the chutes for loading onto the cars. The herds were first grazed and watered some miles outside of town and then driven into the shipping pens to await their turn for loading. Great care was taken to keep the animals away from the residential part of town; had they escaped, it could have led to loss of life for citizens and cattle both. Although the constant bawling and odor of the cattle, the shunting of cars, and the scream of locomotive whistles may have been music to the ears of speculators and others whose fortunes depended on the "evils of the trade," it meant misery to those citizens unconnected with the cattle business. (Courtesy Kansas State Historical Society.)*

86. *This woodcut depicting the loading of Texas longhorn cattle at Abilene was published in* Frank Leslie's Illustrated Weekly *on August 19, 1871. The problems of loading the half-wild cattle aboard railroad cars is obvious. Sometimes animals with a spread of horns in excess of seven feet were pushed toward the ramps, but more often every effort was made to separate these out and saw off their horns before they could do any damage. Although the trip up the trail was hazardous and must have been adventuresome, little has been written about the men who accompanied the cattle to market and fed and watered them. To keep the cattle on their feet, the men had to be ready to go among them, and, should an animal—or a man—go down and create panic in the herd, there was little chance of survival among the thrashing hooves. (Courtesy Kansas State Historical Society.)*

87. *McCoy's famous Drover's Cottage was erected at Abilene in 1869 and later was dismantled and removed to Ellsworth, where it competed with the Grand Central Hotel and other establishments. It was a three-story, one-hundred room hotel with a laundry and a dining room. Its broad veranda was a favorite meeting place for the cattle dealers, drovers, and ranchers who sealed many bargains there over iced drinks and a friendly "seegar." (Courtesy Kansas State Historical Society.)*

88.   On May 8, 1871, during an important debate over the resignations of members of the Abilene city council, G. L. Brinkman moved that the resignation of two members of the council be considered at once, and the motion was unanimously carried. Brinkman then moved that the resignations of Messrs. L. Boudinot and Carpenter be accepted, and that motion also carried. S. A. Burroughs, however, who had voted against the motion, immediately left the chamber without permission. Brinkman motioned that the marshal be ordered to "compel [Burroughs's] attendance." Hickok brought Burroughs back, but he immediately left again. Brinkman again motioned that he be brought back, and this time Hickok carried him in across his shoulders and prevented him from escaping a second time.

At Topeka, where the story became the joke of the week, the noted artist Henry Worrall promptly executed this sketch. It was photographed by Knight, and copies of it were widely distributed, but the copy from which this print was made is the only one I know of that still exists. An important facet of this drawing is Worrall's depiction of Hickok with moustache and goatee, suggesting that this was his current fashion.

Mayor McCoy, who had chosen Wild Bill as marshal after Marshal Smith's murder, had a stormy relationship with his fellow council members, and frequently he was accused of illicit dealings with gamblers and others. It was during one of his absences from the city in 1871 that the council, headed by its president J. A. Gauthie, decided to dismiss Wild Bill, having already made up their minds that the cattle season of 1872 should take place elsewhere. (Minute Book of the City Council of Abilene, 64, 105-107, Manuscript Division, KSHS. Photograph courtesy Kansas State Historical Society.)

89a, b. *Benjamin Thompson, best known as "Ben," was born on November 11, 1842, at Knottingley, Yorkshire, England, the son of William and Mary A. Thompson. His family emigrated to the United States in 1851 and settled in Austin, Texas, where Ben grew up. During the Civil War he served with the Second Texas Cavalry and was wounded in action. His marriage to Catherine Moore was beset in its early years by difficulties with his wife's relatives. He shot and wounded his wife's brother, Jim*

Moore, when he caught Moore striking her, and spent two years in the state penitentiary as a result.

A noted gambler and gunfighter, Ben was known in most of the Kansas cowtowns. In 1871 he had an interest in the Bull's Head Saloon, in partnership with Phil Coe, another Texan. Some have said that Hickok accused the pair of cheating their own fellow Texans, but the evidence is not conclusive. Ben left Abilene toward the end of the season and only heard the details of the Hickok-Coe shoot-out secondhand.

Hickok and Coe had their final showdown outside the Alamo Saloon on October 5, 1871. Rumors all through the summer had intimated that they would eventually fight, and Coe had been heard to say that he would get Wild Bill "before the frost."

According to the family Bible, Phil was born in July, 1839, the son of Philip and Elizabeth Coe of Gonzales County, Texas. During the Civil War he enlisted in and deserted from several Texas regiments, having served in various commissioned and noncommissioned ranks. Following the war he joined Ben Thompson in Mexico to fight with Maximilian's forces, and the pair were later engaged in gambling pursuits together. When Ben left Abilene, Phil took over the Bull's Head Tavern. Plate 89b is a photograph from the Coe family album.

On March 11, 1884, in company with his friend John King Fisher, Thompson visited the Vaudeville Variety Theatre in San Antonio, Texas, where King proposed to act as a peacemaker in a dispute between Thompson and the gamblers Joseph C. Foster and William H. Simms. The three had fallen out, and Fisher had hoped that he could prevent a shoot-out. Unfortunately, Foster and Simms had no such conciliatory intentions, and both Thompson and Fisher, with no chance to defend themselves, were gunned down by hidden accomplices of Simms and Foster. When the smoke cleared, Ben Thompson, one of the most feared gunfighters in Texas, was dead. (Floyd Benjamin Streeter, Ben Thompson, 23, 79, 89, 196. Plate 89b courtesy L. Crozier and Chuck Parsons.)

90.

This tintype of John Wesley Hardin was found in one of his albums that came into the possession of his cousin Joseph Hardin. Written beneath the picture was the information that it had been made at Abilene in 1871. There were no photographers in Abilene that year, however, so presumably it was made at Junction City—possibly by A. P. Trott—or at some other place on the cattle trail.

Born on May 26, 1853, at Bonham, Texas, Wes Hardin was the son of a Methodist preacher, but his early life in post-Civil War Texas provoked the more violent side of his nature, and the antics of the hated Texas State Police did little to placate his aggressive tendencies. Whether he was a homicidal maniac or just a victim of circumstances is beyond the scope of this study, but it is true that he killed his first man in 1868, and by 1871 the number had risen to twelve, seven of whom he had killed on his way from Texas to Abilene that year. He killed another man in 1871 after his arrival in Abilene.

To boost a fading ego, Wes penned a most remarkable autobiography in 1895, in which he claimed to have worked the "roadagents' spin" on Hickok and disarmed him. He also suggested that Hickok was a long-haired coward. In a letter dated 1888, however, Hardin had written that "no braver man [than Hickok] ever drew breath."

The murder of a sheriff in Texas and his involvement in various feuds made Hardin a much wanted man. He was finally captured in 1877 and sentenced to twenty-five years in the state penitentiary. In jail he studied law and was a model prisoner. His voluminous letters to his wife Jane bear testimony to his intention to change his ways. His wife died on November 6, 1892, a little more than a year before his release from prison on February 17, 1894.

Although some of the fire was still there, Hardin was indeed a changed man, but most people knew him only through his reputation. He married a young girl named Callie Lewis on January 8, 1895, but she soon left him and refused ever to see him again. Many believe she was infatuated with the legend but unable to reconcile to the man.

His ungovernable temper made him unpredictable, and his law practice was not a success. He was arrested and accused of robbing a faro game in El Paso's Gem Saloon on April 16, 1895, and was fined twenty-five dollars. He continued to sink lower and became an embarrassment to his friends. But he still had a reputation as a gunfighter, and that may have been the cause of his death. On August 19, 1895,

as he stood drinking at the bar of the Acme Saloon, he was shot through the head by John Selman, who, according to some sources, gave him no chance to draw. (John Wesley Hardin, The Life of John Wesley Hardin, *5, 44-45, 141-42; Leon Metz,* John Selman, Gunfighter, *170-81; photograph courtesy Robert E. McNellis.)*

91a, b. *Photograph 91a of Wild Bill was taken about 1871 and belonged to J. B. Edwards. It is the one discussed in the introduction. The very old copy from which*

The last photo made of
Wild Bill, in 1876.

this version was made is uncredited. Most of those I have seen bear Forney of Abilene's imprint and were made from the Edwards original. I examined a carte de visite some years ago that showed Trott's imprint, and it was this print that was used in the April 10, 1926 issue of Saturday Evening Post to illustrate a fictionalized account of the life of one Fred E. Sutton. A retouched version of the photograph exists, mounted on a card and bearing the inscription "Sincerely J. B. Hickok"—the signature apparently a facsimile taken from the Ellis County document reproduced as Plate 77a. Hickok is wearing trousers similar to those depicted in the Fort Harker photograph shown as Plate 64, and the bow tie could be the same one.

A portrait photographer who examined this photograph and compared it with other Hickok portraits expressed the opinion that the studio lighting was misplaced. Instead of heightening facial shadows to mold the face, the photographer used too much top lighting, creating the impression of a weak chin when, in fact, Hickok's chin line was very firm. Shown as 91b is a badly retouched version from the original Rose Collection, incorrectly dated 1876. (Plate 91a courtesy the Dickinson County Historical Society, Abilene, Kansas; Plate 91b courtesy the Noah H. Rose Collection, Western History Collections, University of Oklahoma Library, Norman.)

CHAPTER FIVE

Showman
(1872-1874)

The Wild West Show is an established part of American folklore and owes its origin to various people, notably Phineas T. Barnum, who purchased fifteen buffalo from C. D. French, an expert rider and lasso artist, and exhibited them in 1843. The exhibition was a failure, but Barnum and others learned from the mistake.[1]

Legend has it that Wild Bill organized a show in June, 1870, at Niagara Falls, New York, but no such spectacle took place at the falls that year. The actual date was August, 1872, and, although Hickok was master of ceremonies, the actual promotion was the work of Colonel Sidney Barnett, son of Thomas Barnett, a Niagara Falls museum owner. In an effort to attract more visitors to the Canadian side of the falls, the Barnetts decided to present a spectacle of Indians, buffalo, and the already romanticized American "cowboy" and Mexican "vaquero." Some of Barnett's agents reached Wichita, and Barnett himself appeared at Fort McPherson, where he engaged John B. ("Texas Jack") Omohundro to appear with some of his Pawnee Indian friends. However, the United States government refused to let the Indians cross the international border, and so Omohundro also refused to take part.

Undaunted, Barnett finally engaged a number of Sac and Fox Indians, and while he was in Kansas City, Missouri, he met Wild Bill, who was soon persuaded (for an undisclosed fee) to act as master of ceremonies. The "Grand Buffalo Hunt" took place on August 28 and 30, 1872. Despite much publicity, the reaction of the audience was mixed. Nonetheless, it clearly established that a properly organized spectacle of this kind could be profitable.[2]

Returning to Kansas City, Hickok spent most of the summer there and became a familiar figure at the racetracks and in various gambling saloons. In September the annual Kansas City Fair took place, and Wild Bill joined the

140

crowds that thronged the grounds. On September 27 an estimated thirty thousand people were in attendance when some Texans approached the bandstand and demanded that the band play "Dixie." Many of the bystanders protested, and some of the Texans pulled their pistols. At that moment Wild Bill stepped forward and ordered the bandmaster to stop. As many as fifty pistols were "presented at William's head, but he came away unscathed."[3]

Whether Hickok had also attended the fair the day before is unclear; it is part of his legend that on that day he stopped the James gang from robbing the till. In reality, they got away with the money and escaped unharmed.[4]

From Kansas City, Hickok is believed to have gone to Springfield, Missouri, where he had many friends from the war. Unconfirmed reports suggest that he remained there all through the winter, but not until March can his presence there be clearly established. In the meantime, an incident took place in Nebraska that was to have serious repercussions for the people involved, and years later Hickok's reputation was to suffer because of it. Late in November, 1872, three leaders of the Cut-off band of Oglala Sioux were shot to death, and the name "Wild Bill" was mentioned in connection with the murders.

The Indians were Whistler, Badger, and Handsmeller, and it was believed that they had been murdered somewhere near the Republican River and that their bodies had been removed to the place where they were later found. At first the killings were said to have resulted from a dispute between the Sioux and the Pawnees, but later it was learned that white men were responsible. The army was called upon to investigate the matter, and on January 7, 1873, Captain Charles Meinhold, commanding Company B, Third Cavalry, left Fort McPherson, accompanied by two commissioned officers and fifty-one enlisted men.

Peter, the chief of the Pawnees, denied that his men were responsible, although the theft of horses from his tribe by the Sioux would have been sufficient reason for the Pawnees to attack them. Lieutenant Frederick Schwatka (later to be the first man to explore the Yukon River to its full length), acting on information from settlers, visited a farmer named Samuel C. Gaste, who stated under oath that he had been hunting buffalo on December 3 when he came upon two men hunting wolves. When he asked the men to give him directions to the nearest water, they attempted to send him out of his way. His suspicions aroused, he chose his own route and came across the bodies of the three Indians and two dead ponies. Wagon tracks and the manner in which the bodies were lying convinced him that they had been dumped on the spot. One of the men he recognized as John ("Jack") Ralston, who belonged to what was called "Wild Bill's Outfit."

The army laid the blame squarely at the feet of the mysterious "Wild Bill and his Outfit," and for a time it was claimed that the Wild Bill was Hickok. Later investigations, however, have revealed that the man responsible was one William Kress, known locally as "Wild Bill of the Blue [River]" to distinguish him from Wild Bill Hickok. With Kress was Newton Moreland, who was seen riding Whistler's horse soon afterward. Later Ralston made a statement before Barclay White, superintendent of Indian affairs, describing how he and Kress had decided to "waltz" (kill) the Indians "or they will waltz us, tonight." They waited until the Indians were helping themselves to coffee and other supplies and shot the three of them dead.

Settlers in the area feared for their lives, and reprisals were expected against the whites, but none came. With time, the horror of the killings and the anger against those responsible for them were forgotten, which, perhaps, explains why Doc Carver made an irresponsible claim to have shot the Indians himself and used the story for theatrical purposes. But no one took him seriously. Besides, many had welcomed Whistler's death; he and his band had been responsible for a number of attacks against the whites, and they were believed to have been involved in the murder of the Nelson Buck surveying party in 1869.[5]

Early in March, 1873, it was reported that Hickok had been murdered at Fort Dodge, the victim of an assassin. The telegraph wires across Kansas crackled with various versions of the affair, and his friends and enemies speculated upon the truth. The Kansas City *Times* reported that "for the benefit of the Kansas City papers," Hickok had announced in the Springfield (Missouri) *Advertiser:* "I hereby acknowledge that I am dead." Chiding Wild Bill for lying in such a "grave-way," the editor later quoted the Springfield *Times*'s reaction: "We suppose he means dead drunk." In Leavenworth, Kansas, while bemoaning the passing of Wild Bill, a frontier "hero" who would be hard to replace, another editor prophesied that "writing obituary notices of him is likely to furnish occupation for Western journalists as yet unborn." It was Hickok, however, who finally took the matter seriously and dispelled the rumors by writing to the editors of two Saint Louis papers (and perhaps others), informing them that he was very much alive.[6]

Sometime during the spring and summer of 1873, Buffalo Bill Cody, who had just abandoned his partnership with Ned Buntline, wrote to Wild Bill and later discussed with him the financial and other advantages of joining him and Omohundro in their theatrical troupe. Cody went to Fort McPherson during the summer and enjoyed a week's hunt in company with E. B. Overton and several other Easterners. Whether they met Hickok at the fort or at Omaha is uncertain, but the press carried a report stating that Cody would soon reorganize his company and take it to Europe and that Hickok would accompany them. The European trip never materialized, but Hickok did join the "Combination," and in September, 1873, he took to the boards as an actor with a unique role—himself.[7]

Cody's Combination, with Wild Bill as an important member, toured extensively during the period from September, 1873.to March, 1874. Hickok did not enjoy his part of the bargain. Complaints that he did not take either the productions or himself and his companions seriously led to friction. It was also alleged that he overloaded his pistols so that Indians or "supers" who were supposed to whoop and drop dead before his deadly aim suffered from powder burns and continued jumping about. It was also claimed that he threatened the spotlight operator because he gave Cody more attention than he gave Wild Bill and that, when the unfortunate man did turn the light full upon him, Hickok yelled to him to turn the "blamed thing off" because it almost blinded him. Early in the season he had caused a minor uproar—but won the audiences' hearts—by refusing to drink cold tea and tell stories: "Either I get real whisky or I ain't tellin' no story!"[8]

By the time the company reached Rochester, New York, Hickok had had enough. He parted amicably from his two friends, each of whom presented him with five hundred dollars and a fine pistol,[9] bidding him to "make good use of it among the 'Reds.'"[10] After a brief sojourn in New York, it was reported, he joined a rival production. Tiring of it, he soon left, but when he learned that an actor had been engaged to play "Wild Bill," he returned and wrecked the show. Convinced at last that he was not cut out for the stage, Hickok set course for the one place where he felt free and where he really belonged—the West.

92

For many years the original of this photograph hung in the home of Wild Bill's
sister Lydia, at Oberlin, Kansas. Later it was brought to Troy Grove, where Horace
Hickok allowed me to examine it. The image is on glass and is about whole-plate
(8'' x 6'') size. Although it is very sharp, its sepia color makes the original appear
faded. Horace said that it was made in the early 1870s, and the length of Wild Bill's
hair would support this conclusion.

This portrait is perhaps the most interesting and thought-provoking of all the
photographs of Wild Bill, for, despite the length of the exposure, the expression is
clear and bears a hint of the tragedy that awaited him. Contemporary press reports
and statements credited to his friends lend support to the legend that Hickok did
indeed have a premonition of his death. (Courtesy the late Horace Hickok.)

145

93

Buffalo Bill Cody, Ned Buntline, and Texas Jack Omohundro, in a relaxed pose, during the 1872-73 season of the Combination. Buntline, whose real name was Edward Zane Carroll Judson, adopted his pen name following a short career at sea in his youth. A notorious womanizer, he was credited with at least four marriages and was involved in a number of disputes over women. In 1869 he was well established as a dime novelist, and it has been claimed that, although he originally sought Hickok as his hero, he found Cody instead. His Buffalo Bill: King of the Bordermen, *first published in 1869, was the source for the drama* Scouts of the Prairie, *featuring himself, Cody, and Omohundro, that was first staged in December, 1872, in Chicago.*

Cody, at first reluctant to tread the boards, soon realized that he enjoyed it and persuaded Texas Jack to join him. Jack was not very happy at first; like most frontiersmen, he disliked crowds and preferred a life in the open air, but he let himself be persuaded. Although he gained some fame during this time, he never achieved the lasting reputation of Cody and Hickok. Born on July 26, 1846, in Virginia, he served in the Confederate army during the Civil War and afterwards worked as a cowboy in Texas (thus his sobriquet). Later he appeared in Nebraska, where he spent much of his time with the Pawnees and became one of the few white men of the time to win their trust.

During the period he was with Cody, Jack fell in love with and married the female lead of the show, Josephine Morlacchi, and the few short years they had together were very happy. Jack died, a victim of pneumonia, on June 28, 1880, and his wife was grief stricken. She died on July 23, 1886. (Albert Johannsen, The House of Beadle and Adams and Its Dime and Nickel Novels, *2:168; Herschel C. Logan,* Buckskin and Satin, *4, 188-93.)*

Buffalo Bill   Ned Buntline   Texas Jack.

147

a

b

c

94 a–c. *Reproducible copies of 94a are rare, and the men at either end of the group have not been positively identified. Some have suggested that the man at Hickok's feet is Colorado Charlie Utter. Recent research, however, and the discovery of the photograph reproduced as 94b (which clearly shows both men in civilian dress) suggest that they are Elisha Green and Eugene Overton. The man in the center of 94b is thought to be named Scott, a New York hatter. In July, 1873, the Omaha papers reported that Cody, Omohundro, Green, Overton, and Scott were in town following a successful hunt. En route East, the group found time to be photographed by Currier, a local photographer, and it is believed that 94b is a copy of that photograph. According to the March 12, 1914, issue of the Denver Post a copy of the photograph shown as 94a was presented to Buffalo Bill, and the figures were identified as Green, Hickok, Cody, Omohundro, Overton. The original was probably made in one of the eastern cities where the troupe appeared in late 1873 or early 1874.*

Shown at 94c is Wild Bill separated from his companions. It is by far the best version of this pose, for it has not been retouched, only scuffed and scratched. It was discovered in an album compiled between 1863 and 1900 by the artist James Earl Taylor, an illustrator with Frank Leslie's Illustrated Weekly. The original is a tintype measuring approximately 2¾'' x 6½'', which suggests that the original plate was perhaps 14'' x 10'' Unfortunately, Taylor left no written comment on the photograph, so it is not known whether he cropped Cody and his friends from the plate or whether that had already been done when he received it. Plate 94c is reproduced in reverse to obtain the correct image.

The weapons displayed by the group are typical of the period. One of the "tenderfeet" carries an up-to-date Smith and Wesson "American" revolver in his belt, and the scouts are armed with Colt percussion revolvers. Omohundro carries two Colt Navy revolvers, and Cody has an 1860 Army revolver thrust into his belt. Strong magnification by the Smithsonian has failed to determine Hickok's pistol: it is either a Colt Navy or a Smith and Wesson "American" with a carved ivory butt. Hickok, Green, and Overton are holding "prop" weapons; Cody and Omohundro are armed with Remington Rolling Block rifles.

A close examination of Wild Bill's belt buckle suggests that it is identical to the one in Plate 96a, into which he also has thrust a bowie-type knife. (Gary L. Roberts to the author, September 29, 1980; Omaha, Nebraska, Daily Republican, July, 1873; Paula J. Fleming, National Anthropological Archives, Smithsonian Institution, to the author, October 2, November 21, and December 9, 1980. Plate 94a courtesy the Western History Collection, Denver Public Library. Plate 94c courtesy Smithsonian Institution, National Anthropological Archives, Washington, D.C.)

95.

During the period that Wild Bill traveled with Buffalo Bill's Combination, Fred G. Maeder produced several plays under the general title Scouts of the Plains, and this illustration is from the program of one of them. Evidently it owes little or nothing to Buntline's Buffalo Bill: King of the Bordermen. It is printed on a light green paper in black type; printed on the reverse are selected incidents in the lives of the three scouts. Although Cody was the principal character, Wild Bill's career was given the most space (the long quote was taken from General Custer's Galaxy articles which were later published in his book My Life on the Plains in 1874).

When questioned about the penciled comment ("I was not in the hall but I don't think Jim was there."), Ethel Hickok said that, although she did not recall anyone making any specific remarks, perhaps the individual who wrote on the card had not recognized "Uncle Jim," or perhaps Hickok had not appeared in that particular performance. (Courtesy Ethel Hickok.)

THE PROGRAMME

ON THE TRAIL.

The Scouts of the Plains !

BUFFALO BILL,
TEXAS JACK,
WILD BILL.

Dramatic Company, Tribe of Indians

PROGRAMME FOR THIS EVENING.

Fred. G. Maeder's Famous Western Drama,

Buffalo Bill!

KING OF THE BORDER MEN !
In Three Acts.

Buffalo Bill..............(by Hon. Wm. F. Cody)..........Buffalo Bill **Himself**
Texas Jack.........(by Mr. J. B. Omoaundro)........Texas Jack **Himself**
Wild Bill................(by Mr. J. B. Hickok)................Wild Bill **Himself**
THE OLD VET, an 1812 Pounder, (Author of the Drama).......FRED G. MAEDER
Snakeroot Sam, Down on Snakes................................Walter Fletcher
Col. Jake McKandlass...Alfred Johnson
Alf Coyle, a Renegade..W. S. MacEvoy
Murty Mullins, The Sentinel..................................R. Wheeler
Perkins, a Landlord..E. N. Watson
Flipup...W. G. Specke
Stockwell..E. Cunningham

INDIANS.

Fire Water Tom, a Drunken Red...J. V. Arlington
"Oof"	"Oof"	"Oof"	"Oof"
Raven Feather, a Sioux Brave...Jas. Johnson
Big Maple, a warrior .... } By the
Little Elk, the same...................................... } Tribe
White Arrow, the same..................................... } from the
Little Panther, the same.................................. } Plains
Ma-no-tee, the Princess of the Ogallalla Soux..............Esther Rubens

LADIES.

Lillie Fielding, the Rose of the Plains...................Lizzie Safford
Lottie Fielding, the Wild Bud.............................Eliza Hudson
Mrs. Fielding...Jennie Fisher
KITTY MULDOON, an Irish Girl...........................RENA MAEDER

b

c

96a–c. *Wild Bill in buckskins, perhaps his most famous portrait. The two original prints of this photograph that I have examined have been* carte de visites, *and both are credited to Wilbur Blakeslee of Mendota, Illinois. One is owned by the Kansas State Historical Society, the other by the Nebraska State Historical Society. Each bears the printed inscription: "W. Blakeslee, Photographer, Elmwood, Ills. Negative Preserved." "Elmwood, Illinois" has been lined out and the legend "Opposite Passenger House, Main St., Mendota, Ill." has been added.*

Various writers have dated this photograph 1865, 1867, 1869, and 1871, and its similarity to the pen portrait of Wild Bill by Nichols has not been overlooked: "Bill stood six feet and an inch in his bright yellow moccasins. A deer-skin shirt, or frock it might be called, hung jauntily over his shoulders, revealed a chest whose breadth and depth were remarkable. . . . his small round waist was girthed by a belt which held two of Colt's navy revolvers."

Hickok visited Mendota in March, 1869, on his way to his mother's home at Troy Grove, and the local press mentioned his stopover at the Passenger House, so it is just possible that Blakeslee made the plate at that time. The late Vincent Mercaldo, however, expressed the opinion that the photograph was made at Fort McPherson in 1871, although no evidence has been found to place Hickok at the fort that year. An examination of the photograph—and the length of Wild Bill's hair—suggest that perhaps this photograph was made during the period he appeared as a member of Buffalo Bill's Combination (1873-74) and that his apparel is stage costume. The 1851 U.S. Army belt buckle is identical to that shown in Plate 94c, and the addition of the plains-style butcher or bowie knife in the belt with his two Colt 1851 model Navy revolvers is more theatrical than practical.

Plate 96b is from the original Noah Rose Collection and is reproduced to illustrate the disastrous results of too much retouching and constant recopying. Plate 96c is a combination of 96a and the photograph of an "unknown miner" purported to be Hickok. The differences are obvious, however, when the two photographs are reproduced to the same scale—Hickok is a head taller than his "namesake." (The full story of Blakeslee's alleged connection with this photograph was told in the Mendota Reporter, July 13, 1977. Plate 96a courtesy the Kansas State Historical Society; 96b courtesy the Western History Collections, University of Oklahoma Library; 96c [miner] courtesy the Western History Collection, Denver Public Library.)

97.

This photograph of Wild Bill Hickok, Texas Jack Omohundro, and Buffalo Bill Cody has been credited both to Rockwood and to Gurney & Son of New York. An original print in my collection, made about 1880, is uncredited but carries the imprint "Copyright Secured." A search by the Library of Congress indicated that no Hickok photographs were actually copyrighted, but it did reveal three photographs, copyrighted between 1890 and 1903, of the various monuments erected over Hickok's grave.

The place where this photograph was made has also been disputed. John M. Burke, Cody's manager, recalled in later years that the photograph was made at Syracuse, New York, during the latter part of Hickok's appearance with the Combination. Each of the scouts wears clothing representative of the style of both the 1970s and the 1870s. Hickok's familiar fur hat can be seen resting on the table. (Jerry L. Kearns, Head Reference Section, Prints and Photographs Division, Library of Congress, to the author, April 19, 1977.)

155

98a–c. *This portrait of Wild Bill, discovered in a scrapbook of clippings in the William E. Connelley Collection of the Denver Public Library, came from an unidentified newspaper. It is credited to Gurney & Son, New York. Dated 1873-74, it depicts Hickok in show costume, complete with his favorite fur hat. In reproducing, as 98a, this poor newspaper reproduction (the only known copy), I also include a partly retouched version as 98b and, as 98c, a copy executed in oil. (Plates 98a and b courtesy the Western History Collection, Denver Public Library.)*

156

157

158

HEROES OF THE PLAINS

OR

Lives and Wonderful Adventures

OF

WILD BILL, BUFFALO BILL, KIT CARSON,
CAPT. PAYNE, CAPT. JACK, TEXAS
JACK, CALIFORNIA JOE,

AND OTHER

CELEBRATED INDIAN FIGHTERS, SCOUTS, HUNTERS AND GUIDES

INCLUDING

A TRUE AND THRILLING HISTORY OF GEN. CUSTER'S FAMOUS
"LAST FIGHT" ON THE LITTLE BIG HORN,
WITH SITTING BULL.

BY J. W. BUEL,
Author of "Border Outlaws," "Legends of the Ozarks," and other popular works.

PROFUSELY ILLUSTRATED.

NEW YORK. :
PARKS BROTHERS,
338 Broadway,
1882.

99a, b. *Plate 99a is a cut of Wild Bill taken from the 1882 edition of J. W. Buel's* Heroes of the Plains, *and the full illustration, which is in color, is shown as 99b. It is reproduced here because it is believed that the artist made the cut from an original photograph—as he did with Cody's portrait below—but copies of the Hickok photograph have not yet come to light. (Courtesy Kansas State Historical Society.)*

100.

This photograph of Wild Bill, complete with fur cap and white silk tie, has rarely been published without retouching. This print is one of the best known, and a careful examination reveals that he is wearing skintight kid gloves, fashionable at the time. Dated 1873-74, the portrait has often been credited to Rockwood, although it is also possible that Gurney & Son made the original plate. Some writers have gone so far as to suggest that this was Hickok's last portrait and have given its location as Deadwood—although why Hickok should wear a fur hat in the height of summer is not explained.

A number of paintings depicting Hickok dressed in this coat have appeared in recent years; in each the artist has made the mistake of adding colored facings to the jacket. In fact they were silk, or some other shiny material, and of the same color as the coat—black or gray. (Courtesy Western History Collections, University of Oklahoma Library.)

a

101a–j *(pages 162-65).* *George Rockwood of New York is credited with making three plates of Hickok, but original photographs bearing his imprint are rare. Plate 101a bears his name, whereas 101b is credited to the Majilton Photographing Company of Philadelphia. Copies of this portrait were also sold by Gurney & Son of New York. The woodcut reproduced as 101c was made from 101b and was used*

WILD BILL.

LIFE AND MARVELOUS ADVENTURES
—: OF :—
WILD BILL,
THE SCOUT,
By J. W. BUEL, OF THE ST. LOUIS PRESS,
ILLUSTRATED WITH NUMEROUS ENGRAVINGS.

BEING A TRUE AND EXACT HISTORY OF ALL THE SANGUINARY COMBATS AND

HAIR-BREADTH ESCAPES OF THE MOST FAMOUS SCOUT AND SPY AMERICA EVER PRODUCED.

WILD BILL.

A marvelously exciting book, full of daring adventures and wonderful escapes among the Indians and lawless white men of the Far West.
PAPER COVERS, PRICE 25 CENTS.
Sent free to any address on receipt of price.
N. D. THOMPSON & CO., Publishers,
520, 522 and 524 Pine St.,   ST. LOUIS, MO.

b

c

as an advertisement for Buel's first account of Hickok published in 1879-80. The illustration at 101d is an imaginative attempt: evidently the artist was unaware that Hickok was seated for the original photograph.

The portrait shown as 101e, perhaps one of Hickok's best known, was made from the original plate owned by Vincent Mercaldo, who credited it to Rockwood. The gradual loss of emulsion is obvious in the left-hand corner of the print. Plate 101f is reproduced only to illustrate the mutilation of the inexpert retoucher and comes from the original Rose

d

J. B. HICKOK. (WILD BILL.)

Clegg,   DIAMOND STUDIO.   Victor, Colo.

e

WILD BILL HICKOK, Marshal at Abilene, Kansas, in 1871.

f

Collection. Perhaps the most
bizarre effort seen is in 101g,
which is a straightforward
transplant—Hickok's head
has been placed on a body
that once belonged to
Buffalo Bill (191h). It is
credited to White and dated
1892. White was one of
several photographers of
the era who delighted in a
style of "retouching" that
was more like a mutilation.

An examination of the
famous Cross painting of
Hickok shown at 101i shows
that it, too, is based on 101b,
and despite the date "1874"

g

h

i

j

it was painted many years afterwards. The cut at 101j is also based on 101b and is best described as "romantic." (Plates 101d and f courtesy the Western History Collections, University of Oklahoma Library; Plate 101c courtesy Chuck Parsons; Plates 101g and h courtesy Buffalo Bill Historical Center, Cody, Wyo.; Plate 101i courtesy the Thomas Gilcrease Institute of American History and Art, Tulsa, Okla.; Plate 101j courtesy the Western History Collection, Denver Public Library.)

102a–c. *The show bill reproduced as 102a is typical of those pasted up around town to announce the forthcoming appearance of Buffalo Bill's Combination. This version appeared at Keokuk, Iowa, in April, 1874, by which time Hickok had already left the troupe and returned west through New York. It is historically important because the woodcut portraits of the three scouts are made from photographs, but only those of Cody and Omohundro have so far been found. The poster shown as 102b is interesting because it suggests that Hickok was an even bigger attraction at that time than Cody. This was probably so because, despite his theatrical fame, Cody had only a limited frontier reputation, whereas Hickok was known nationwide—if not as Hickok, certainly as Wild Bill. The illustration at 102c is an artist's impression of what the original photograph probably looked like.*

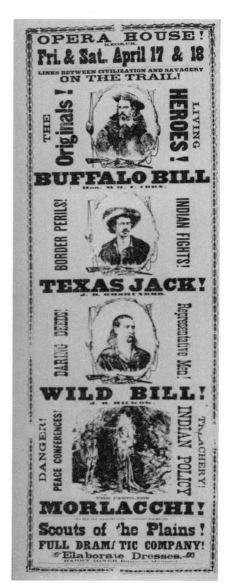

a

c

OPERA HOUSE!
KEOKUK.
Fri. & Sat., April 17 & 18

LINKS BETWEEN CIVILIZATION AND SAVAGERY
ON THE TRAIL!

DARING DEEDS!

Representative Men!

WILD BILL!
J. B. HICKOK.

IN A NEW AND THRILLING DRAMA OF WESTERN BORDER LIFE.

Scouts of the Plains!

FULL DRAMATIC COMPANY!
☞ Elaborate Dresses. ☜
HARRY MINER, Business Manager

MERRIHEW & SON, SHOW PRINTERS 183 N. 3d STREET, PHILADA.

b

103.

Buffalo Bill, from a "Woodburytype" photograph made in England about 1887, when his "Wild West" appeared, first in London and then in the provinces. Queen Victoria was so impressed by the spectacle that she had several private viewings, and, on her public appearance at the arena in London's Earl's Court, she amazed and delighted the Americans when she rose from her seat as "Old Glory" was borne proudly past and bowed—the first time since the Declaration of Independence that a British monarch had recognized the American flag.

Cody never used the word "show" in connection with his "Wild West," and although its content changed greatly in later years, the essential "cowboys, cavalry and Indians" theme remained; it is to him that credit goes for stimulating a worldwide interest in the part factual, part mythical Old West. (Don Russell, Lives and Legends of Buffalo Bill, *330. Photograph courtesy Colin Crocker.)*

104. *The "Deadwood Stage," from a "Woodburytype" made in London in 1887. The driver is Tom Duffey, who once drove the coach on the Cheyenne to Chugwater run, and the bearded figure seated at the rear is John Y. Nelson. Unlike the Hollywood versions, this coach is pulled by six mules (two of them are out of camera range), as were many of the early-day coaches. Only later were horses employed, and then only over certain routes. Mules were noted for their endurance, particularly in rough country. Horses, however, were faster, and they were used on routes best suited to them.*

Cody purchased the coach in 1883 from Luke Voorhees, superintendent and part-owner of the Cheyenne and Black Hills Stage Line, and ran it for years in his "Wild West." In Europe, kings and queens were pleased to ride in it, and it remained the favorite of the many thousands who witnessed the passing of an era. Even today the stagecoach is an important ingredient in any Western film worthy of the name. (Agnes Wright Spring, Cheyenne and Black Hills Stage Routes, *163, 359. Photograph courtesy Colin Crocker.)*

CHAPTER SIX

A Legend in His Time
(1874-1876)

Wild Bill's movements when he returned to the West early in 1874 are obscure, for only scattered mention of him is found in the press. Early that year
it was reported that he was at Yosemite and would soon return to Denver to
join Buffalo Bill Cody, Texas Jack Omohundro, and a number of others on
a buffalo hunt.

A comparison of Hickok's known movements with those of Cody and
Omohundro reveals that on July 17, Cody was at Omaha, where he stayed at
the Metropolitan Hotel, but that a day or so later he was on his way to
Denver, and on July 25 he was at North Platte. Omohundro, however, was
still in the East and only arrived in Denver, accompanied by his wife, in early
August. As for Wild Bill, he was reported to be on a train that passed through
North Topeka on July 18. A reporter managed to get a word or two from him
and learned that he was expecting to meet Bill Cody and Texas Jack at
Cheyenne. At Kansas City he was hired as a scout by a party of "about
twelve English Lords and noblemen" and on July 22 was in Cheyenne. He
left there on July 27, presumably with the same party, to go hunting.[1] Between trips to Saint Louis and Kansas City, Hickok continued to make Cheyenne his base for the next two years. Stories of gunfights with rivals or attempts on his life by relatives of those he had sent to "warmer climes" (particularly Phil Coe) were common, but no reports of Wild Bill engaging in such
activities—let alone firing off a pistol—have been found. Rather, he was a
man out of his element. For the tenderfeet, who crowded into Cheyenne's
saloons and gambling dens before trips to the Black Hills in search of gold,
his tongue-in-cheek stories of the great wealth to be had in caves "up north"
must have stirred their spirit of adventure. Of his own exploits there are press

comments enough to verify that he boosted his own legend and convinced some editors that he should be taken at his word.[2]

Despite fleeting glimpses of him in the press in 1875, almost the whole of that year is still cloaked in mystery. Indeed, the only definite reference to Hickok is found on June 17, when he was charged with vagrancy. A warrant for his arrest was issued the same day. Curiously, the case never came to court, and old-timers questioned on the subject could offer no reason for the charge, concluding that perhaps it was his reputation as a violent man that was responsible.[3]

Hickok's marriage to Agnes Lake Thatcher on March 5, 1876, seemed to be a turning point, for after a short honeymoon at her Cincinnati home he was back in Cheyenne preparing to organize an expedition to the Black Hills which he hoped would earn him enough money to send for his wife. Hickok's "Black Hills and Bighorn Expedition" was to be organized in Saint Louis, and, according to circulars he distributed to the press, it would start from there on May 16 and proceed to Cheyenne by way of Jefferson City, Sedalia, Kansas City, Lincoln, and Omaha. Each man had to outfit himself with a good rifle and two hundred rounds of ammunition, a rubber blanket, two woolen blankets, and six months' provisions. Tents to accommodate two, four, or seven men were also required. From Cheyenne the expedition would go either to Sidney or to Custer City and thence on to the Bighorn country. As well as the cost of provisions, each man was to pay Wild Bill $25.00 to $33.65.[4]

But things did not go according to plan. The press intimated that "Idaho Bill" and C. C. Carpenter were organizing a similar expedition to leave on April 3, and, in a letter to his family, Agnes wrote that James (she always called him by his true name) had "put off the trip until the first of June" but gave no explanation. On June 8 he was again in Cheyenne, as was Colorado Charlie Utter, who had made several appearances there since early March, organizing his own proposed Black Hills Transportation Line and a "pony express." By early June, however, the pair had decided to join forces, and when Charlie and his brother Steve set out for Deadwood on or about June 27, Wild Bill was with them.[5]

The party made a brief stop at John Hunton's ranch at Bordeaux on June 30 and spent some time talking with him. On the morning of July 1 the travelers set off for Laramie.[6] It is reported that by the time the party arrived at Deadwood on or about July 12, it had increased in number and included several prostitutes, among them Calamity Jane. "White-Eye Jack" Anderson also claimed to have accompanied Hickok on that trip, and he recalled that Hickok did little socializing, being more concerned with his daily pistol practice.[7]

Hickok's presence in Deadwood aroused much interest, particularly among those who knew him only by reputation — a notoriety equally divided between the heroic figure of *Harper's* and a Western "desperado." Old friends were eager to renew his acquaintance, among them California Joe, whose appearance of unkempt benevolence never seemed to change. Like Wild Bill, he was a good friend but a bad enemy.

Wild Bill spent less than a month in Deadwood, yet, if we were to believe even half the stories of his exploits during that period, the time would seem to have been much longer. While Utter busied himself in preparation for his proposed transportation line and pony express, Hickok got in a little prospecting. Cynics have suggested that the only prospecting he actually did was in seeking suitable partners for the next game of poker, but on his own word we must give him the benefit of the doubt: "I never was as well in my life but you would laughf [*sic*] to see me now," he wrote to his wife on July 17. "Just got in from Prospecting[.] will go away again to morrow. Will write In the morning."[8]

Back in Cincinnati, Agnes eagerly awaited the mail carrier, for, true to his word, James did write to her as regularly as he was able. On August 7 she received a letter from him that she sent on to Troy Grove. It would be some days before she received the letter dated August 1 — his last.[9]

Built on land that was still a part of the vast Sioux reservation, Deadwood was illegal. It was also lawless in other ways; the lure of gold, quick profits, and easy pickings from the tenderfeet who flocked to it had attracted pimps, gamblers, and prostitutes eager to relieve them of their hard-earned "dust." It was not long before residents and transients alike appreciated the need for some kind of order. Wild Bill's name was bandied about as a possible candidate for marshal, though there is no real evidence to support the belief that he was offered the job.

Leander P. Richardson was one of the few who left recollections of Wild Bill during this period, but his accounts seem designed more for an audience avid for heroes than for those seeking historical fact. Writing in 1877 he described a buckskin-clad Hickok, saying he was "the most courageous man I had met on the plains," adding that he was noted for his "rapidity of motion, courage, and certainty of aim," as well as for his ability to control his associates. Seventeen years later, however, Richardson changed his description of Hickok's "two silver-mounted revolvers" to one of an old Army revolver and wrote that the "control" was in the hands of Utter, "but I was never quite

able to decide to my own satisfaction whether Utter amused or awed him."
Richardson arrived in Deadwood on August 1, so his recollection of Hickok
is based upon the evidence of a single day—and his own imagination.[10]

That Hickok knew his enemies were determined to get him is no longer
disputed, yet his coolness while awaiting their move was remarkable. His
friends tried to persuade him to leave town for awhile and join California
Joe on a buffalo hunt, but he refused. To Wild Bill that would have been
tantamount to admitting fear, or worse, cowardice. "Those fellows over across
the creek have laid it out to kill me," he retorted, "and they're going to do
it or they ain't. Anyway, I don't stir out of here, unless I'm carried out."[11]

On the afternoon of Wednesday, August 2, he sat in on a poker game in
Nuttall and Mann's No. 10 Saloon with Charlie Rich, Carl Mann, and Captain
William Rodney Massie, a former Missouri River pilot. Several times during
the game Hickok asked Rich to let him have his wall seat, but Rich refused,
and Wild Bill, facing the front door and conscious of the one in the rear,
continued to play uneasily. At about 3:00 P.M. a small, nondescript individual
entered the front door, meandered up to the bar, and then eased himself
behind Hickok. There was a shot and the shout, "Damn you, take that!"
Massie looked up, puzzled by the noise and the sudden numbness of his left
arm, just in time to see Hickok fall sideways from his stool. Suddenly he was
aware of a man with a smoking pistol, who began yelling to everyone to get
out of the place.

The murderer, after snapping his pistol at the bartender and at the
others who had remained, rushed out the back door and tried to mount a
horse, but the saddle turned under him, and he fled to a butcher's shop,
where he hid. By that time a furious crowd was in pursuit, and the ringing
cry, "Wild Bill has been shot! Wild Bill is dead!" echoed up and down the
street. When the murderer was captured, he was identified as Jack McCall, a
laborer, who sometimes went by the name of Bill Sutherland and had been
employed in various activities since his arrival in Cheyenne some weeks earlier. Only the night before, he had played cards with Hickok and had lost;
on the morning of his murder, Hickok had insisted on lending McCall the
money for his breakfast.[12]

There was talk of a lynching, but McCall was swiftly borne away and
locked up in a cabin. A coroner's jury was impaneled and concluded that
Hickok had died instantly from the effects of a pistol ball fired by the accused. Massie, meantime, had been to a doctor; the fatal bullet had passed
through Hickok and was lodged in his wrist. It was reported years later that
he had never had it removed, and there it remained when he died in 1910.[13]

174

According to Ellis T. ("Doc") Peirce, a barber with a little surgical knowl-edge who served as coroner and arranged for a coffin, Hickok "bled out" quickly. Peirce was then able to prepare him for burial. Utter took care of the actual funeral arrangements, and during the late afternoon a notice was printed by the *Black Hills Pioneer* announcing the time of the funeral as 3:00 P.M. on the next day. A great crowd attended, and someone carved this epitaph on a tree stump at the head of the grave: "A brave man; the victim of an assassin—J. B. (Wild Bill) Hickock, aged 48 years; murdered by Jack McCall, August 2, 1876."

In the meantime, a number of citizens had organized a proper trial for McCall, and, with Judge W. L. Kuykendall presiding, it opened at 9:00 A.M. on August 3. McCall's defense was in the hands of Judge Miller, and the prosecution was undertaken by Colonel George May. Despite overwhelming evidence of murder, the jury accepted McCall's plea that he had killed Hickok in revenge for the death of a brother slain by Wild Bill in Kansas. He was found not guilty and released.

McCall, however, did not linger in town for long. Friends of Wild Bill, particularly Utter and California Joe, made it clear that, given any excuse, they would kill him. He fled to Cheyenne and then to Laramie City, where he was arrested by a deputy U.S. marshal. A United States commissioner ruled that since the Deadwood trial was illegal McCall would have to face trial in a federal court. The trial was held at Yankton, Dakota Territory, from December 4 to December 6, and McCall was found guilty. On January 3, 1877, he was sentenced to be hanged. Several petitions were drawn up plead-ing for his life, but President Grant refused to intervene. On March 1, with the single choking cry of "Oh God!" as he plunged through the trap, Jack McCall joined his victim in death.[14]

Three years later, Wild Bill's remains were removed to a new resting place on Mount Moriah, and his grave has since been visited by many thou-sands of people. The real Wild Bill Hickok belongs to history, but his legend is very much a part of that fabulous era of fact and fiction, romance and nostalgia, that belongs to "The Wild West."

105.   *The location of the Metro-politan Billiard Hall shown in this faded and retouched photograph has not been established. Both Cheyenne and Denver are given as possible sites, and the year as possibly 1874 or 1875. The crowd is alleged to include such notables as "Doc" Middleton, one of the most famous horse thieves in Nebraska history, and "Bloody Dick" Seymour, friend and employee of Charlie Utter. The fifth man from the left, standing beside the aproned figure (who was known as "Doc" Howard) and holding a cane in his right hand, is reputed to be Wild Bill. The identification is based pri-marily on his stance, mode of dress, and long hair; strong magnification has failed to bring up the features, thus making positive identification impossible. (Courtesy the Western History Collection, Denver Public Library.)*

106a, b *(pages 178-79).   Original prints of Plate 106a, taken in 1875, have not been found, but a number of retouched versions are known. The Kansas City* Journal-Post *of December 5, 1926, credited the photograph to D. D. Dare of Cheyenne, Wyoming, who was in business there during the period Hickok frequented the place and probably was the original photographer. Shown at 106b is a woodcut from the photograph executed by the "Photo. Eng. Co.," which appeared in Buel's* Heroes of the Plains. *In 1915, Major John M. Burke, Cody's publicity agent, informed a reporter from the El Paso* Herald *that he*

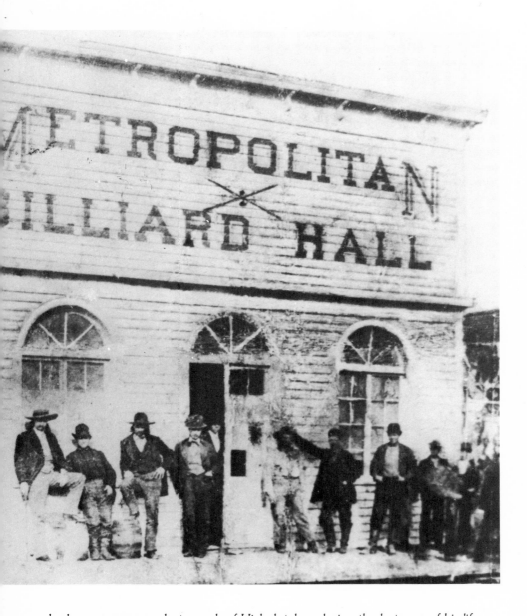

had come across a photograph of Hickok taken during the last year of his life. On November 2, he was quoted as saying that the portrait showed "a more mellow, thoughtful, professor-like cast of countenance than this great law and order marshal of the west showed as the fearless, dashing spy, guide, scout and ranger in more youthful days." It is believed that Burke was referring to this portrait. Certainly the face is a striking contrast to the Henry portrait of seven years before (Plate 55c).

Hickok's appearance in Cheyenne in 1874 was unheralded, according to

most authorities, and the inimitable Alfred Henry Lewis produced a most amusing account, a classic of its kind. Having disguised his appearance and armed himself with a heavy rosewood billiard cue (for his rheumatism), Hickok "concluded to creep about" in order to take in a "friendly" view of the city. At the Gold Room he found he was being cheated and promptly declared war on the management. Once the customers realized who he was, they proceeded to "go through the doors and windows in blocks of five." Wild Bill then walked off with the pot. In fact there was an incident in the Gold Room, but Hickok was not the main participant. For most of his stay in the city he was not in any difficulty. Surprisingly, therefore, on June 17, 1875, he was charged with vagrancy, and a warrant for his arrest was issued the same day. This was never served, however, and following his death the docket entry bore the terse comment: "Deft. dead. Dismissed."

Hickok's reputation obviously bothered some people, and Doc Howard

JAMES B. HICKOK
(WILD BILL)

recalled that Wild Bill was once stopped on the street by the redoubtable T. Jeff Carr and ordered out of town. Hickok stared him out and remarked: "Jeff Carr, when I go, you'll go with me," and walked away. Mrs. Annie Tallent met Hickok in Cheyenne in 1875 and thought him a perfect gentleman, an opinion shared by many.

It was during the period between 1874 and 1876 that reports circulated of Hickok's alleged eye trouble. No conclusive evidence has come to light, but informed opinion is that he was afflicted with trachoma, a common complaint on the frontier. (Alfred Henry Lewis, "How Mr. Hickok Came to Cheyenne," Saturday Evening Post, March 12, 1904; Laramie County Clerk of Court, Criminal Appearance Docket, 2:230, June 17, 1875-June 12, 1876, Wyoming State Archives, Cheyenne; Rosa, Wild Bill, 267-71; Annie Tallent, The Black Hills, 100.)

107a–c. *Agnes Lake Thatcher (107a), from a photograph made in the late 1860s that was discovered in Dodge City. By her own statement she was born on August 24, 1832, but her place of birth—whether Cincinnati, Ohio, or Alsatia—has not been established. She met and married William Lake Thatcher when she was a young girl. Thatcher was a circus man who, for professional reasons, was known as William or*

Bill Lake. Their daughter, Emma (107b), was born on February 22, 1856, and, like her parents, grew up to love and take part in the circus.

The Lakes toured with circuses in the United States and Europe before forming their own troupe and touring both eastern and western states. Agnes was widowed when Bill was murdered at Granby, Missouri, on August 21, 1869, but she kept the show on the road. In July, 1871, her Hippo-Olympiad and Mammoth Circus reached Abilene, and there she met Wild Bill. For the next five years they kept up a correspondence and met infrequently. She later told his family that she had "loved James for three years" before she married him but had delayed the event until her daughter was married.

Following Hickok's death she declared, "It is impossible for a human

b

c

being to Love any better than what I did him. I can see him Day and night before me. The longer he is Dead the worse I feel." Although her name was linked romantically with at least one other man, she never remarried, and until her death on August 21, 1907 (thirty-eight years to the day after Lake's murder), she preferred to be known as "Mrs. Hickok" and it was no secret that she still mourned him.

Her daughter, Emma, maintained family tradition and became a famous equestrian with Buffalo Bill, joining his English tour in 1887, when Plate 107c was made. Her future husband, Gil Robinson, recalled that when he first met Wild Bill he had been surprised; instead of a "desperado" he had found a man with the manners of a perfect gentleman and the looks of a preacher. During the period she traveled with Buffalo Bill, and perhaps later, Emma insisted upon being billed as "Emma Hickok." (Rosa, Wild Bill, 234-41, 308. Plates 107a and b courtesy the Kansas State Historical Society; Plate 107c from a stereoscope card copyrighted in 1889 by Underwood & Underwood and sold in the United States by Strohmeyer & Wyman, New York.)

108. *On the morning of March 5, 1876, Wild Bill and Agnes Lake Thatcher were married at the home of S. L. Moyer, who, with his wife Minnie, witnessed the ceremony performed by the Reverend W. F. Warren. Although the marriage was a happy one, Reverend Warren wrote in the remarks column of his church register, "I don't think the[y] meant it." Agnes's letters and statements in later years disprove his hasty conclusion, however.*

Following the ceremony the couple journeyed to Cincinnati and spent a two-week honeymoon there. They agreed that Hickok should return west and head for the Black Hills; once he had made a strike, he would send for her, and they would settle down.

The original marriage certificate is believed to be in a private collection. The version reproduced here is from a photostat owned by the Connecticut State Library. The photographs of Wild Bill and his wife are pasted to the back of the certificate, the originals having been cut out and removed. Only an examination of the original certificate will show if these photographs are identical to the originals. Agnes declared her age to be forty-two, and Wild Bill gave his as forty-five. (Courtesy Connecticut State Library, Hartford.)

182

109. *Cheyenne in the 1860s and 1870s was not only a railroad terminus but also the base for a large number of freighting enterprises and the headquarters of the Cheyenne and Black Hills Stage Line. The illustration shows a typical freight train of about 1876, about to move off from Eddy Street. The huge loads the wagons carried made eight, ten, and even more mules or oxen a necessity, especially when crossing country where roads were either unknown or little more than rough tracks. "Mule skinners" were a tough breed and as hard to handle as their teams. (Courtesy Wyoming State Archives, Cheyenne.)*

110. *Despite its frontier reputation, Cheyenne by the mid-1870s, as this photograph from a stereoscope shows, was largely civilized and rapidly becoming respectable. This view is looking east on Seventeenth Street from Ferguson and is dated 1875 (Courtesy Wyoming State Archives.)*

183

111a, b. *Martha Jane Cannary, alias Calamity Jane, dressed in an unfamiliar manner in 111a and in more familiar raiment in 111b. Her early life is still a mystery, but she was a familiar figure in the Fort Laramie area in the early 1870s as a "sporting" woman at E. Coffey and Cuny's Trading Post. Stories of her exploits are many, and some defy even a cursory examination, yet she emerges as one of the truly colorful characters of the Old West.*

Calamity Jane

In her later years she described a relationship with Wild Bill that many considered a ludicrous claim; the appearance in 1941 of an alleged "diary" and other papers sought to establish a marriage between them. A woman even came forward claiming to be the child of the marriage. A marriage certificate was produced — a page torn from a Bible and dated September 1, 1870, and allegedly written by the same Reverend W. F. Warren, then "enroute to Abilene," who married Hickok and Mrs. Lake six years later. According to the "diary" (written in the form of letters to the daughter) Calamity claims that Hickok divorced her in order to marry Mrs. Lake, but no papers have been found to verify either a marriage or a divorce.

When the daughter, a Mrs. Jean Hickok McCormick, started to receive nationwide publicity (she even persuaded the United States government to give her a pension on the strength of the diary), she was confronted by a member of the Hickok family and, after close cross-examination, finally admitted that she had not been born until 1880— four years after Hickok's death.

At the time of the alleged marriage Hickok was at Junction City, Kansas, actively engaged as a deputy U.S. marshal; where Jane really was at this time has yet to be positively established. When she died at Terry, South Dakota, on August 1, 1903, her friends insisted that she be taken to Deadwood for burial, and they also invented a deathbed wish: "Bury me next to Bill." To complete the hoax, they changed the date of her death to August 2, 1903—27 years to the day after Hickok's murder. Although the true date of her death now appears on her tombstone, she still lies twenty feet from Hickok, sharing an intimacy in death that did not exist in her lifetime.

112.

Photographs of Colorado Charlie Utter are unknown, and this drawing by Janet Lange, published in 1869 in the French magazine Le Tour du Monde, must be accepted with reservation. Born in 1838 near Niagara Falls, New York, Charlie (sometimes spelled Charley), grew up in Illinois but later moved to Colorado, where he earned a local reputation as a trapper and guide. When and where he first met Hickok is not clear, but by 1876 they were firm friends. When Charlie organized his Pony Express service between Cheyenne and Deadwood and went there to set things up, Hickok joined him.

Utter's contemporaries noted that he held Hickok in high regard, and it was he who arranged for Wild Bill's funeral and paid for the plot that became his final resting place. Many years later someone tried to sell Hickok's remains to a museum, on the pretext that the grave had not been paid for. Charlie rushed to Deadwood and proved ownership, and leaving no one in any doubt that if anything happened to the grave, the responsible parties would be answerable to him.

Utter's last years are shrouded in mystery. He made intermittent appearances in various parts of the West, but he is believed to have ended his days in obscurity in Panama, where for a time he operated a drugstore. (Agnes Wright Spring, Colorado Charlie, Wild Bill's Pard, 3, 96-103, 122-24, 127. Photograph courtesy the Western History Collection, Denver Public Library.)

Joseph ("White-Eye Jack") Anderson and his friend Yankee Judd, photographed at Leadville, Colorado, in 1879. "White-Eye" got his name following an accident: a burning buffalo chip landed in his left eye during a prairie fire; friendly Indians helped him, and he kept his sight, but his eyebrow had turned snow-white.

Anderson claimed to have known Hickok at Fort McPherson in the early 1870s and to have accompanied Wild Bill and Charlie Utter on their trip to Deadwood in 1876. He recalled that Wild Bill kept himself aloof from many of the strangers in the party. Anderson said that Calamity Jane joined the party at Fort Laramie but that Hickok ignored her. During the trip Wild Bill taught him some of the finer points of shooting and practiced daily with a pair of Colt Navy revolvers converted from percussion to .38-caliber rimfire.

The party met Buffalo Bill and a detachment of the Fifth Cavalry at Sage Creek (known as Hat Creek), but Cody and Hickok did not speak, according to Anderson, because they had fallen out some time earlier. Although the newspapers hinted at a difference of opinion, Cody always maintained that Wild Bill remained his firm friend until his death. (Rosa, Wild Bill, 284-87.)

189

115. *Mainstreet, Deadwood, early in 1877. Laid out on April 28, 1876, Deadwood originally consisted of this one street, which weaved around the tree stumps, boulders, and potholes left by early arrivals. Saloons were swiftly followed by general stores and other buildings and dwellings. As the photograph shows, a bank was also of importance, and regular shipments of gold from the diggings were made by way of the Cheyenne and Black Hills Stage Line route. It was the lure of gold that attracted swarms of con men, pimps, prostitutes, and gamblers, as well as some of the most famous men in the west. Its glory is long gone, but the town Deadwood is world famous.*

114 *(left). Deadwood late in 1876, looking north, from a photograph by Stanley J. Morrow. Clearly shown on the right of the photograph is the Senate Saloon, where Wild Bill had an altercation with Tim Brady, allegedly one of the principal figures in the plot to assassinate Hickok. But Brady disappeared, one jump ahead of a deputy U.S. marshal, as did John Varnes, the man implicated by McCall at his Yankton trial. Custer's "last stand" was already a part of folklore, and the saloon named after him was perhaps the first of many.*

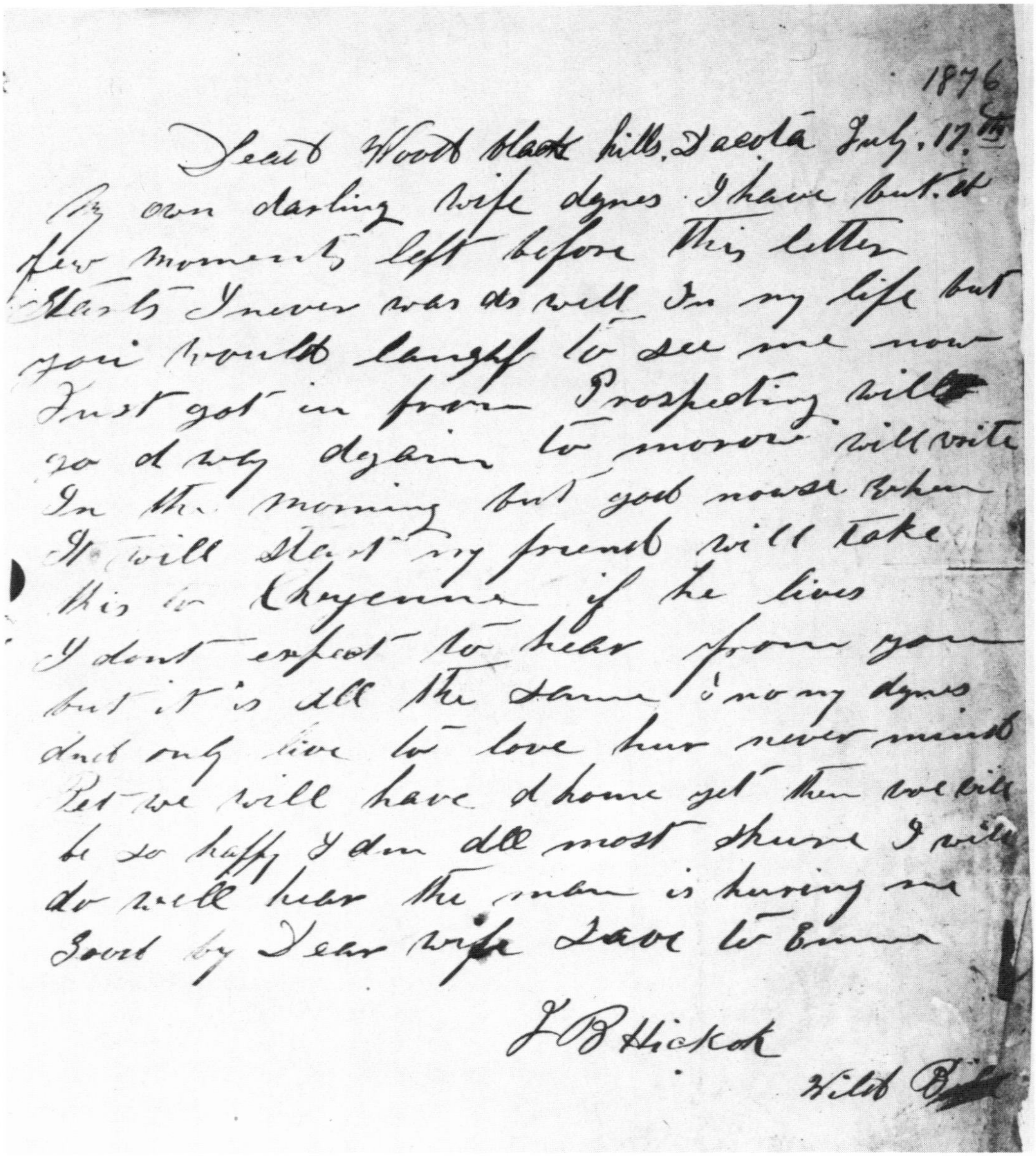

1876

Dear Wood Black hills, Dacota July, 17th
My own darling wife Agnes I have but a
few moments left before this letter
starts I never was as well in my life but
you would laugh to see me now
Just got in from Prospecting will
go a way again to morrow will write
in the morning but god nowse when
it will start my friend will take
this to Cheyenne if he lives
I dont expect to hear from you
but it is all the same o no my Agnes
And only live to love her never mind
Pet we will have a home yet then we will
be so happy I am all most shure I will
do well hear the man is hurring me
Good by Dear wife Love to Emma

J B Hickok

Wild Bill

---

116. *This letter from Wild Bill is one of the few from the period to have survived, although in 1926 Frank Wilstach claimed to have seen one written on August 1, the night before Hickok died, in which Wild Bill alludes to his death and his deep feelings for his wife: "If such should be we never meet again, while firing my last shot, I will gently breathe [the] name of my wife—Agnes—and with wishes even for my enemies I will make the plunge and try to swim to the other shore." The letter reproduced here was in the possession of Hickok's son-in-law Gil Robinson as late as 1926, but its present owner is unknown. (Cited in Wilstach,* Wild Bill Hickok, *282. Photograph courtesy Connecticut State Library.)*

"WILD BILL."

117. *This imaginative woodcut of Wild Bill appeared in Leander P. Richardson's "A Trip to the Black Hills," published in the February, 1877, issue of* Scribner's Monthly. *(Courtesy Chicago Historical Society.)*

118a, b. *Wild Bill's first grave, from a stereoscope produced around 1877 (118a).
The board was erected to reproduce the words carved on the stump against which
it rests. It was an attraction for tourists and others who visited the Black Hills, and
Deadwood in particular. A reproduction of the marker shown at 118b is placed inside
Hickok's present grave by the Deadwood Chamber of Commerce each summer to
attract tourists who, like thousands before them, make annual pilgrimages to see Wild
Bill's last resting place.*

    *Following his burial on August 3, 1876, Wild Bill rested in peace until August 3,
1879, when he was exhumed to be reburied on Mount Moriah. Colorado Charlie
again took care of the arrangements; early on that morning he and some men
removed Hickok to the new grave. Before this second interment, however, they
opened the coffin and were amazed to discover that the body had become petrified.
A contemporary report stated:*

The body at interment weighed about 180 pounds, but upon its removal it weighed not less than 300. There was no odor and no perceptible decay, and it is supposed by those who examined it that petrification had taken place, as it was hard as wood, and returned the same sound as a log when struck with a stick. Everything in the coffin was found just as it was placed there, and the rumor that the grave had been rifled is all bosh. The only article buried with the body was a carbine, and that was in as good a state of preservation as ever. There was no knife or revolvers buried with him as reported, and those who should know say that he never owned a pistol in the Hills. His hair was as glassy and silky as when in life. . . . His moustache was hard, and seemed like his body to have been petrified.

Later it was alleged that Hays City wanted Hickok's remains returned in order to place them outside the local courthouse, for "it is not every man who is qualified to serve as a statue on his own tomb." Perhaps even Wild Bill would have appreciated the macabre humor of the suggestion, for it was also reported that even "the smile on his face [had] become immortal." (Hays City Sentinel, *August 15 and 29, 1879.)*

119.   Moses Embree Milner, better known as "California Joe," from a tintype believed to have been made in Pioche City, Nevada, in 1873, on one of the few occasions when he actually dressed up. Born in Kentucky in 1829, Joe went west and became a skillful trapper and mountain man. He served as a scout in the Mexican War (1846 to 1848) and spent several years in California before establishing a cattle ranch in Oregon. He married and had four sons but later left his family to wander the West. He acquired his alias because of his California connections and should not be confused with the "California Joe" of Berdan's sharpshooters. His reputation as a scout prompted Custer to promote him to chief of scouts for the Washita Campaign, but when Milner was found drunk, Custer promptly demoted him. The pair remained fast friends, nevertheless, and exchanged many letters.

Hickok and Joe held each other in great respect, and Hickok is alleged to have said, a few days before his death, that California Joe and his own pistol were the best friends he had. When Wild Bill was murdered, Joe was "out chasing Indians," and only on his return did he hear of his friend's death. He immediately sought out McCall and suggested that the air might be "rather light" for him and that perhaps he should change his residence. McCall knew that Milner would provoke him into a fight if he could, so he left hurriedly.

Less than two months later, on October 29, as Milner stood talking to friends at Fort Robinson, Nebraska, a man named Newcomb shot him in the back with a Winchester rifle—apparently there had been a long-standing feud between the two men. Newcomb escaped justice. Joe was buried in the post cemetery with full military honors, and his reputation as one of the truly great frontiersmen still survives.

a

120a–c. *Plate 120a, a rare tintype of John Wallace Crawford, was made around 1875. Despite its scratched condition, it is a good likeness of the man who was best known as "Captain Jack, the Poet Scout of the Black Hills." Born in County Donegal, Ireland, on March 4, 1847, Crawford came to the United States as a boy. During the Civil War he served with the Forty-eighth Pennsylvania Volunteers and was wounded several times. In the early 1870s he was well known in Nebraska and at one time was employed as a mail carrier between Sidney and the Red Cloud Agency. An early*

b

invader of the Black Hills, he became a member of the Board of Trustees of Custer City and chief of scouts of the Black Hills Rangers.

In August, 1876, when Buffalo Bill Cody returned east, convinced that there would be little prospect of more Indian fighting, Crawford replaced him as chief of scouts of the Fifth Cavalry. It was Crawford who brought the news of the Battle of Slim Buttes to Fort Laramie, a distance of three hundred and fifty miles that he had covered in less than four days. Crawford later appeared as a member of Cody's (re-formed) Combination and, apart from his writings, became well known as a lecturer. He later developed a great friendship with the Hickok family, but his relationship with Wild Bill remains obscure and is based largely on his much quoted poem "The Burial of Wild Bill."

In 1948 the Crawford family allowed a number of Captain Jack's firearms to be exhibited, and among them was a .31-caliber five-shot Colt 1849 pocket pistol, serial

198

c

number 186213, manufactured around 1860. The weapon is silver-plated and bears
the backstrap inscription·"James B. Hickok"; the butt flat is inscribed "From R. M. & W."
On the right grip is a silver shield on which is engraved "Wild Bill, to Capt. Jack BLACK
HILLS 1876." There is no documentation to prove any real connection with Hickok,
and Crawford himself is thought to have added the shield (120c) in later years.

"R. M. & W." is believed to mean "Russell, Majors & Waddell," but why the
company should present such a weapon to Hickok, an obscure employee in 1860
or 1861, is not explained. By frontier standards the 1849 pocket model was ineffectual
as a "man-killer" but was welcomed as a hide-out gun. (Robert E. McNellis to the
author, February 12 and 25, 1976; Don Russell, Lives and Legends of Buffalo Bill,
240-41, 254-58, 262-63. Plate 120a courtesy Fred Borsch; Plate 120b and c
courtesy Robert E. McNellis.)

121. *This photograph, purportedly of Jack McCall, hangs on the wall of the Old Style Bar at Deadwood, South Dakota, but no real evidence exists to verify the portrait. The man bears little resemblance to the "cross-eyed," "snub-nosed," and "brutish creature" that was the Jack McCall of the national press. This man, on the contrary, looks mature and balanced.*

    McCall was about twenty-five years of age when he reached Deadwood.

122. *President Ulysses Simpson Grant was presented with Jack McCall's plea for clemency. When his plea was declined, McCall was hanged. This photograph, made during Grant's years as a Civil War general, is from a carte de visite credited to E. & H. Anthony, New York.*

He came from Kentucky, where his parents and three sisters still lived. His movements are difficult to trace, partly because he used several aliases. In Deadwood he used the name John McCall when it suited him, or Bill Sutherland, but he usually answered to "Jack." His claim that he murdered Hickok in revenge for a brother shot down by Wild Bill at Hays City was prompted by his defense counsel. Despite a great deal of contemporary and later-day research, it is still not clear why McCall killed Hickok. Many believe he was the tool of others; some think that he attempted, in a drunken stupor, what many others had tried and failed to do: kill Hickok. But rather than confront such a man face to face, McCall shot him from behind.

Allegations of perjury were made against the jury, and because Deadwood was an illegal town on an Indian reservation the authorities were prompted to take action. They again arrested McCall for a legal trial in Yankton. On the night before he died, McCall announced that he would write an account of what really happened, but he destroyed what he had written and took his secret to the grave. (Joseph G. Rosa, Alias Jack McCall.)

Notes

INTRODUCTION

1. William F. Cody, *Life of the Honorable William Frederick Cody*, 71.
2. J. W. Buel, *Heroes of the Plains*, 20.
3. J. B. Edwards Collection, Manuscripts Division, Kansas State Historical Society, Topeka, Kansas (hereinafter cited as KSHS).
4. Ibid., Apr. 20, 1922.
5. Junction City *Weekly Union*, Apr. 4, 1868, and May 1 and 8, 1869.
6. J. B. Edwards Collection, Sept. 30, 1929.
7. Vincent R. Mercaldo to the author, Aug. 12, 1968.
8. Robert Taft Collection, Manuscripts Division, KSHS.
9. Frank A. Root Collection, Manuscripts Division, KSHS.
10. Philadelphia *Evening Bulletin*, Jan. 29, 1910.
11. Gail Marciano, Print Room, the New-York Historical Society, to the author, May 25, 1979.
12. Vincent R. Mercaldo to the author, Aug. 12, 1968.
13. Ibid., July 13, 1968.
14. Mary E. Everhard to the author (1960-61 correspondence). I interviewed Miss Everhard at Leavenworth, Kansas, on Oct. 16, 1965. Unfortunately, I was not able to examine the plate at that time; it was locked in a local bank vault.
15. David R. Phillips and Robert A. Weinstein, *The West: An American Experience*, ix-xiv.
16. The Westerners' *Brand Book*, vol. 3, no. 4 (June, 1946), 24.

CHAPTER ONE

1. The town's name was changed when the citizens learned that there was another and larger Homer in the same state.
2. William Frank Zornow, *Kansas: A History of the Jayhawk State*, 67-68.

3. It has been suggested that Hickok drove stagecoaches, but the company of Russell, Majors and Wardell never ran stages on that route (Dr. John S. Gray to the author, Mar. 24, 1978).

4. Don Russell, *The Lives and Legends of Buffalo Bill,* 41; Howard L. Hickok, "The Hickok Legend," 8, unpublished manuscript, copy in the author's possession provided by Hickok's son, James B. Hickok.

5. Colonel George Ward Nichols, "Wild Bill," *Harper's New Monthly Magazine,* February, 1867, 273-85.

6. Atchison *Daily Champion,* Feb. 5, 1867.

7. For a complete examination of the McCanles incident, see Charles Dawson, *Pioneer Tales of the Oregon Trail and of Jefferson County,* 209-24; William E. Connelley, "Wild Bill—James Butler Hickok: David C. McCanles at Rock Creek," KSHS *Collections,* vol. 17 (1926-28), 1-27; George W. Hansen, "True Story of Wild Bill-McCanles Affray in Jefferson County, Nebraska, July 12, 1861" (with maps, photographs, and sketches by Addison E. Sheldon *et al.*), *Nebraska History Magazine,* vol. 10 (April-June, 1927), 67-146; Levi Bloyd, *Jefferson County History: Rock Creek Station;* Joseph G. Rosa, *They Called Him Wild Bill: The Life and Adventures of James Butler Hickok* (hereinafter cited as Rosa, *Wild Bill*), 34-52.

8. Bloyd, *Jefferson County History.* The Rocky Mountain Dispatch Company used McCanles's West-side ranch until February, 1861, when they left owing him money. The company also had four horses and two sets of harness belonging to him.

9. Dawson, *Pioneer Tales,* 216.

10. The original documents are reproduced in Hansen, "True Story of Wild Bill-McCanles Affray," 107-12.

11. Dawson, *Pioneer Tales,* reproduces a letter from Monroe complimenting him on his efforts, but in the Kansas City (Mo.) *Star,* Nov. 18, 1928, he debunks Hickok and the legendary version of the fight.

CHAPTER TWO

1. Horace D. Hickok to the editor, Topeka *Mail and Breeze,* Sept. 27, 1901.

2. I am indebted to Miss Jo E. Lohoefener, of Oberlin, Kansas, for providing a copy of this letter, which was found among the effects of her great-grandmother Lydia Hickok Barnes some years ago.

3. George W. Hance, "The Truth About Wild Bill," Topeka *Mail and Breeze,* Dec. 20, 1901.

4. Lorenzo's surviving letters were copied for me by Ethel Hickok, in whose possession they remain. In 1965 I examined the Colt Navy revolver, serial number 143098, manufactured ca. 1862-63; it was at that time in the possession of Horace Hickok.

5. Records of the Quartermaster General, 1861-65, National Archives, Washington, D.C.

6. Rosa, *Wild Bill,* 62, 66-68.

7. George A. Root, "Reminiscences of William Darnell," KSHS *Collections,* vol. 17 (1926-28), 508.

8. Diary of Major Albert Barnitz, Second Ohio Cavalry, Barnitz Papers,

Beinecke Library, Yale University; Springfield *Missouri Weekly Patriot,* Aug. 10, 1865; Circuit Court Record, Greene County, Missouri, Book G (1865), 302; Rosa, *Wild Bill,* 72-83, 86.

CHAPTER THREE

1. Hickok's association with Owen can be traced to the early years of the war. Owen was a member of the group that put up Hickok's bail after the killing of Tutt, but he is best remembered under his more famous alias "Captain Honesty"—a *non de plume* hinted at but never disclosed by the editor of the *Patriot,* doubtless to save a much respected citizen embarrassment. Owen died at Springfield in 1872. Records of the Quartermaster General, Reports of Persons Hired (March-December, 1866), National Archives, Washington, D.C.
2. Rosa, *Wild Bill,* 90-91.
3. Ibid., 92; Mrs. Elaine C. Everly, Military Archives Division, National Archives, to the author, Apr. 25, 1978.
4. Lieutenant Colonel Melbourne C. Chandler, *Of Garryowen in Glory,* 2; Mrs. Frank C. Montgomery, "Fort Wallace and its Relation to the Frontier," KSHS *Collections,* vol. 17 (1926-28), 212.
5. Case No. 482, *United States* v. *John Tobin and William Wilson:* Larceny, Records of the District and Territorial Court of Kansas, Record Group 21, Federal Archives and Records Center, Kansas City, Missouri.
6. Elmo Scott Watson (ed.) and Theodore R. Davis, "Henry M. Stanley's Indian Campaign in 1867," Westerners' *Brand Book,* vol. 2 (1945-46), 103; *Weekly Missouri Democrat,* Apr. 16, 1867.
7. Records of the Quartermaster General, Reports of Persons and Articles Hired by Lieutenant Charles Brewster in Camp near Fort Hays, Kansas (April-July, 1867), National Archives.
8. The Records of the District and Territorial Court of Kansas, Record Group 21, Federal Archives and Records Center, Kansas City, Missouri, contain a number of cases involving Hickok as a witness or as a deputy U.S. marshal between October, 1867, and September, 1870. As late as October, 1871, he was called to give evidence in court at Topeka against a man he had arrested a year before (Case No. 998, *United States* v. *John McAllister:* Counterfeiting).
9. For the complete clipping see Rosa, *Wild Bill,* 115.
10. Ibid., 119; Leavenworth *Daily Conservative,* Mar. 17, 1868.
11. Records of the Quartermaster General (1868-69), National Archives.
12. Rosa, *Wild Bill,* 124-28.
13. Mendota (Ill.) *Bulletin,* Mar. 18, 1869.

CHAPTER FOUR

1. Mendota (Ill.) *Bulletin,* Mar. 18, 1896; "'Wild Bill's' Sister," Chicago *Record,* Dec. 26, 1896.

2. Case No. 792, *United States v. Silas Baker and Willard Curtis*, District and Territorial Court of Kansas, Record Group 21, Federal Archives and Records Center, Kansas City, Missouri; Fort Wallace Letter File (Letters Dispatched, 1869), microfilm copy, Manuscripts Division, KSHS.

3. For a complete résumé of the events leading to Whiting's dismissal, and the whole story of Hickok's exploits as a deputy U.S. marshal, see Joseph G. Rosa, "J. B. Hickok, Deputy U.S. Marshal," *Kansas History*, vol. 2, no. 4 (Winter, 1979), 231-51.

4. Rosa, *Wild Bill*, 135-40; Reverend Blaine Burkey, *Wild Bill Hickok: The Law in Hays City*, 5-6.

5. Kansas City (Mo.) *Daily Journal of Commerce*, Aug. 25, 1869, citing the Leavenworth *Daily Commercial*.

6. Lawrence (Kans.) *Daily Tribune*, Sept. 30, 1869.

7. Hickok's marksmanship has been the subject of innumerable magazine and newspaper articles. I discuss some of these feats in *Wild Bill*, 338-49.

8. Records of Fort Hays (Letters Dispatched and Received, 1869), microfilm copy, Manuscripts Division, KSHS; Governor's Correspondence, ibid.

9. Records of Fort Hays (Letters Dispatched, 1869).

10. Leavenworth *Times and Conservative*, Nov. 5, 1869.

11. Records of Fort Hays (Letters Dispatched, 1869).

12. *United States v. Isaac Shindle:* Preliminary Hearing, District and Territorial Court of Kansas, Record Group 21, Federal Archives.

13. Topeka *Daily Commonwealth*, Feb. 8, 1870.

14. Case no. 828, District and Territorial Court of Kansas, Record Group 21, Federal Archives.

15. Rosa, *Wild Bill*, 156-60.

16. Ibid., 157.

17. Case no. 998, *United States v. John McAllister*, District and Territorial Court of Kansas, Record Group 21, Federal Archives.

18. Wayne Gard, *The Chisholm Trail*, 69.

19. Confusion concerning the location of the trail north from Texas, and its official end, is not a modern problem. As long ago as the 1920s old-timers, some of whom had actually traveled along it, could not agree (Stuart Henry, *Conquering our Great American Plains*, 29-31).

20. Minute Book of the City Council of Abilene, microfilm copy, Manuscripts Division, KSHS, 55.

21. Abilene *Chronicle*, Oct. 12, 1871.

22. Gross to Edwards, June 15, 1925, J. B. Edwards Collection, Manuscripts Division, KSHS; Topeka *Daily Commonwealth*, Nov. 25, 1871. This item, headed "Attempt to kill Marshal Hickok," was later published in the Abilene *Chronicle* of Nov. 30, 1871, without any additional comment.

CHAPTER FIVE

1. Irving Wallace, *The Fabulous Showman*, 96-98.

2. Rosa, *Wild Bill*, 162-69; Pawnee Agency Documents, microfilm copy, Nebraska Historical Society, 2:19-20; Denver *Field and Stream*, June 1, 1895.

3. Topeka *Daily Commonwealth*, Sept. 28, 1872.

4. Frank Triplett, *The Life, Times, and Treacherous Death of Jesse James*, 70.

5. Rosa, *Wild Bill*, 207-21.

6. Ibid., 248-49; Kansas City (Mo.) *Times*, Mar. 11 and 13, 1873; Leavenworth *Daily Times*, Mar. 13, 1873; St. Louis *Missouri Democrat*, Mar. 15, 1873; see also Laramie (Wyo.) *Daily Sentinel*, Mar. 5, 1873; and Topeka *Daily Commonwealth*, Mar. 14, 1873, among others.

7. Omaha *Daily Bee*, July 27, 1873.

8. Rosa, *Wild Bill*, 253; Hiram Robbins, "Wild Bill's Humors," undated clipping from the *Arkansaw Traveler*, supplied by Don Russell.

9. The make of the pistols is uncertain. Some sources suggest that they were a pair of .44-caliber Smith and Wesson "American" centerfire revolvers, and others that they were the two .38-caliber center- or rimfire Colt Navy conversions he is believed to have been carrying at Deadwood.

10. Rochester (N.Y.) *Democrat and Chronicle*, Mar. 14, 1874.

CHAPTER SIX

1. Topeka *Daily Commonwealth*, July 21, 1874; Kansas City (Mo.) *Times*, July 19, 1874; Denver *Rocky Mountain News*, July 31, 1874.

2. Joseph G. Rosa, "How Mr. Hickok Really Came to Cheyenne," in *Kansas and the West*, 83-95.

3. Ibid., 93.

4. Cheyenne *Daily Sun*, Apr. 30, 1876; Cheyenne *Daily Leader*, May 3, 1876.

5. Agnes Lake Hickok to Polly Butler Hickok, June 30, 1876; Agnes Wright Spring, *Colorado Charley: Wild Bill's Pard*, 90-93.

6. Pat Flannery (ed.), *John Hunton's Diary*, 2:115-16.

7. Extracts from his original manuscript supplied by his daughter, Mrs. Ellen Anderson Mitchell.

8. Rosa, *Wild Bill*, 288-89.

9. Agnes Lake Hickok to Polly Butler Hickok, Aug. 7, 1876.

10. Leander P. Richardson, "A Trip to the Black Hills," *Scribner's Monthly*, vol. 13 (Feb., 1877), 755; Leander P. Richardson, "Last Days of a Plainsman," *True West*, vol. 13, no. 2 (November-December, 1965), 22-23, 44-45.

11. Richardson, "Last Days of a Plainsman," 44-45.

12. For a complete résumé of Hickok's death and McCall's subsequent trials, see Joseph G. Rosa, *Alias Jack McCall*.

13. Ibid., 15; Raymond W. Thorp to the author, Nov. 15, 1960.

14. Rosa, *Alias Jack McCall*, 27.

Bibliography

I. BOOKS AND PAMPHLETS

Armes, Col. George A. *Ups and Downs of an Army Officer.* Washington, D.C., 1900.
Bloyd, Levi. *Jefferson County History: Rock Creek Station.* Fairbury, Nebr., n.d.
Buel, J. W. *Heroes of the Plains.* New York and Saint Louis, 1882.
Burke's General Armory. London, 1884.
Burkey, Rev. Blaine. *Wild Bill Hickok the Law in Hays City.* Hays, Kans., 1973.
Chandler, Lt. Col. Melbourne C. *Of Garryowen in Glory—The History of the Seventh United States Cavalry.* Washington, D.C., 1960.
Cody, William F. *Life of the Honorable William Frederick Cody, Known as Buffalo Bill, the Famous Hunter, Scout and Guide: An Autobiography.* Hartford, Conn., 1879.
Connelley, William Elsey. *Quantrill and the Border Wars.* Cedar Rapids, Iowa, 1909.
————. *Wild Bill and his Era.* New York, 1933.
Custer, Elizabeth Bacon. *Following the Guidon.* New York, 1890.
Custer, George Armstrong. *My Life on the Plains.* New York, 1874.
Dawson, Charles. *Pioneer Tales of the Oregon Trail.* Topeka, Kans., 1912.
Dictionary of American Biography. Vol. 13. New York, 1928.
Ebbutt, Percy G. *Emigrant Life in Kansas.* London, 1886.
Edwards, J. B. *Early Days in Abilene.* Abilene, Kans., 1940.
Frost, Lawrence A. *The Custer Album.* Seattle, Wash., 1964.
————. *General Custer's Libbie.* Seattle, Wash., 1976.
Gard, Wayne. *The Chisholm Trail.* Norman, Okla., 1954.
Hall, Richard. *Stanley: An Adventurer Explored.* London, 1974.
Hardin, John Wesley. *The Life of John Wesley Hardin.* Seguin, Texas, 1896.
Harmon, Edith Andrews. *Another Man Named Hickok.* Mendota, Ill., 1973.
————. *Pioneer Settlers of Troy Grove, Illinois: A History of the Hickok Family.* Mendota, Ill., 1973.
Henry, Stuart. *Conquering Our Great American Plains.* New York, 1930.
Hunton, John. *John Hunton's Diary.* Edited by L. G. "Pat" Flannery. 3 vols. Lingle, Wyo., 1956-60.

Johannsen, Albert. *The House of Beadle and Adams and Its Dime and Nickel Novels: The Story of a Vanished Literature.* 2 vols. Norman, Okla., 1950.

Kansas and the West: Bicentennial Essays in Honor of Nyle H. Miller. Topeka, Kans., 1976.

Lamar, Howard R. (editor). *The Reader's Encyclopedia of the American West.* New York, 1977.

Logan, Herschel C. *Buckskin and Satin.* Harrisburg, Pa., 1954.

McClernan, John B. *Slade's Wells Fargo Colt.* Hicksville, N.Y., 1977.

McLintock, John S. *Pioneer Days in the Black Hills.* Deadwood, S.Dak., 1939.

Metz, Leon. *John Selman, Gunfighter.* Norman, Okla., 1980.

Otero, Miguel Antonio. *My Life on the Frontier.* 2 vols. New York, 1935.

Phillips, David R., and Robert A. Weinstein, *The West: An American Experience.* Chicago, 1973.

Pride, W. F. *The History of Fort Riley.* Privately Printed, 1926.

Root, Frank A., and William Elsey Connelley. *The Overland Stage to California.* Topeka, Kans., 1901.

Rosa, Joseph G. *They Called Him Wild Bill: The Life and Adventures of James Butler Hickok.* 2d ed. Norman, Okla., 1974.

Russell, Don. *The Lives and Legends of Buffalo Bill.* Norman, Okla., 1960.

Spring, Agnes Wright. *Cheyenne and Black Hills Stage and Express Routes.* Glendale, Calif., 1949.

———. *Colorado Charley, Wild Bill's Pard.* Boulder, Colo., 1968.

Streeter, Floyd Benjamin. *The Complete and Authentic Life of Ben Thompson: Man with a Gun.* New York, 1957.

Tallent, Annie D. *The Black Hills; Or the Last Hunting Ground of the Dakotahs.* Saint Louis, Mo., 1899.

Utley, Robert M. (editor). *Life in Custer's Cavalry: Diaries and Letters of Albert and Jennie Barnitz, 1867-68.* New Haven and London, 1977.

Verckler, Stewart P. *Cowtown Abilene, The Story of Abilene, Kansas (1867-75).* New York, 1961.

Wallace, Irving. *The Fabulous Showman.* London, 1960.

Webb, W. E. *Buffalo Land.* Cincinnati, Ohio, 1872.

Wilstach, Frank Jenners. *Wild Bill Hickok—The Prince of Pistoleers.* New York, 1926.

Zornow, William Frank. *Kansas: A History of the Jayhawk State.* Norman, Okla., 1957.

II. MAGAZINES AND ARTICLES

Connelley, William Elsey. "Wild Bill—James Butler Hickok: David C. McCanles at Rock Creek," Kansas State Historical Society *Collections,* vol. 17 (1926-28).

Forrest, Col. Cris. (editor). "Wild Bill's First Trail. As He Told It," *DeWitt's Ten Cent Romances,* no. 10 (December, 1867).

Hance, George W. "The Truth About Wild Bill," Topeka (Kans.) *Mail and Breeze,* December 20, 1901.

Hansen, George W. "True Story of Wild Bill—McCanles Affray in Jefferson County,

Nebraska, July 12, 1861" (with supporting articles by Addison E. Sheldon and William Monroe McCanles), *Nebraska History Magazine,* vol. 10, no. 2 (April-June, 1927).

Lewis, Alfred Henry. "How Mr. Hickok Came to Cheyenne: An Epic of an Unsung Ulysses," *The Saturday Evening Post,* vol. 176, no. 37 (March 12, 1904).

Montgomery, Mrs. Frank C. "Fort Wallace and Its Relation to the Frontier," Kansas State Historical Society *Collections,* vol. 17 (1926-28).

Nichols, Colonel George Ward. "Wild Bill," *Harper's New Monthly Magazine,* vol. 34, no. 201 (February, 1867).

Old West, vol. 1, no. 4 (Summer, 1965), "Wild Bill's Rifle" (anon.).

Preston, Paul. "Wild Bill, the Indian-Slayer: A Tale of Forest and Prairie Life," *De-Witt's Ten Cent Romances,* no. 3 (July, 1867).

Richardson, Leander P. "A Trip to the Black Hills," *Scribner's Monthly,* vol. 13 (February, 1877).

Root, George A. "Reminiscences of William Darnell," Kansas State Historical Society *Collections,* vol. 17 (1926-28).

Rosa, Joseph G. "J. B. Hickok, Deputy U.S. Marshal," *Kansas History,* vol. 2, no. 4 (Winter, 1979).

————. "George Ward Nichols and the Legend of Wild Bill Hickok," *Arizona and the West,* vol. 19, no. 2 (Summer, 1977).

————. "Was Wild Bill photo taken here?" Mendota (Ill.) *Reporter,* July 13, 1977.

————. "How Mr. Hickok Really Came to Cheyenne," *Kansas and The West,* Kansas State Historical Society, 1976.

Watson, Elmo Scott (editor), and Theodore R. Davis. "Henry M. Stanley's Indian Campaign in 1867," The Westerners' *Brand Book,* vol. 2 (1945-46).

The Westerners' *Brand Book,* vol. 3, no. 4 (June, 1946) ["Campfire Embers" citing a description of Hickok by the phrenologist DeLester Sackett].

III. NEWSPAPERS

Where only one or two references were made to a newspaper, the actual dates are given; in all other instances the months or years checked are shown.

Abilene (Kansas) *Chronicle,* 1870 and 1871.
Atchison (Kansas) *Daily Champion,* February 5, 1867.
Atchison (Kansas) Weekly *Free Press,* March 2, 1867.
Austin (Texas) *Democratic Statesman,* October 12, 1871.
Austin (Texas) *Weekly State Journal,* October 26, 1871.
Burlingame (Kansas) *Chronicle,* March 28, 1868.
Cheyenne (Wyoming) *Daily Leader,* 1874-77.
Cheyenne (Wyoming) *Daily News,* October 7, December 3, 1874.
Cheyenne (Wyoming) *Daily Sun,* 1874-76.
Chicago (Illinois) *Daily Record,* December 26, 1896.
Deadwood (Dakota Territory) *Black Hills Pioneer,* 1876-77.
Deadwood (Dakota Territory) *Black Hills Times,* 1879.
Denver (Colorado) *Rocky Mountain News,* 1873-77.

El Paso (Texas) *Herald*, November 2, 1915.
Hays City (Kansas) *Railway Advance*, 1867-68.
Hays City (Kansas) *Sentinel*, August, 1879.
Junction City (Kansas) *Daily* and *Weekly Union*, 1866-71 and 1876.
Kansas City (Missouri) *Star*, November 18, 1928.
Laramie (Wyoming) *Daily Sentinel*, 1873.
Lawrence (Kansas) *Daily Tribune*, 1868-69.
Leavenworth (Kansas) *Daily Bulletin*, February 13, 1867.
Leavenworth (Kansas) *Daily Commercial*, 1867-69.
Leavenworth (Kansas) *Daily Conservative*, 1867.
Leavenworth (Kansas) *Times and Conservative*, 1867-72.
Mendota (Illinois) *Bulletin*, March 18, 1869, and April 11, 1873.
Omaha (Nebraska) *Daily Republican*, July, 1873.
Philadelphia (Pennsylvania) *Evening Bulletin*, January 29, 1910.
Rochester (New York) *Democrat and Chronicle*, 1874.
Saint Louis (Missouri) *Weekly Missouri Democrat*, 1867 and 1873.
Springfield (Missouri) *Missouri Weekly Patriot*, 1865-67 and 1872.
Topeka (Kansas) *Daily Commonwealth*, 1870-71.
Topeka (Kansas) *Capital*, August 30, 1908.
Topeka (Kansas) *Mail and Breeze*, September-December, 1901.
Topeka (Kansas) *State Record*, 1869-70.

IV. MANUSCRIPTS AND OTHER MATERIALS

Abilene (Kansas) Minute and City Council Records Books, 1870-72, microfilm copy, Manuscripts Division, Kansas State Historical Society, Topeka.
Anderson, Joseph F. ("White-Eye"). Manuscript in the possession of his daughter, Mrs. Ellen Anderson Mitchell, Fresno, California.
Barnitz, Major Albert. Diary for 1865, Beinecke Library, Yale University, New Haven, Connecticut.
Bell, William, to Frank A. Root, October 19, 1905. Manuscripts Division, Kansas State Historical Society.
Blake, Herbert Cody, to Robert Taft (1933 correspondence). Robert Taft Collection, Manuscripts Division, Kansas State Historical Society.
Carr, General Eugene A. "Carr's Campaign of 1868-69." Manuscript in the possession of James T. King.
Connelley, William Elsey. Collection of letters, clippings, manuscripts, bound copies of his Hickok manuscript, and other typed copies of letters and books, together with a scrapbook, Western History Division, Denver Public Library.
District and Territorial Court Records, Record Group 21, Federal Archives and Record Center, Kansas City, Missouri.
Governor's Correspondence (1868), Manuscripts Division, Kansas State Historical Society.
Gross, Charles F., to J. B. Edwards (1922-26), Manuscripts Division, Kansas State Historical Society.

212

Hansen, George W., to J. B. Edwards, September 30, 1929. Manuscripts Division, Kansas State Historical Society.

Hardin, John Wesley, to his wife Jane, June 24, 1888, copy on file at the San Marcos, Texas, Library.

Hersey, Timothy F., to J. B. Edwards, January 5, 1905. Manuscripts Division, Kansas State Historical Society.

Hickok, Howard L. "The Hickok Legend," unpublished manuscript, copy in the collection of Joseph G. Rosa.

Hickok, James Butler, letters written to his family from Kansas (1856-58), in possession of his niece Ethel Hickok, Troy Grove, Illinois.

Hickok, James Butler, letter to his sister Lydia, dated Springfield, Mo., July 8, 1862, in possession of Jo Lohoefener, Oberlin, Kansas.

Hickok, Lorenzo Butler, letters written to his family from Rolla, Missouri, in 1863, in possession of his niece Ethel Hickok, Troy Grove, Illinois.

National Archives, Washington, D.C.:

Fort Hays Letter File (1867-69), microfilm copy, Manuscripts Division, Kansas State Historical Society.

Fort Wallace Letter File (1867-69), microfilm copy, Manuscripts Division, Kansas State Historical Society.

Records of the Quartermaster General, 1861-69.

Abstract Accounts, Third Auditor of Accounts of Captain R. B. Owen, A.Q.M., U.S.A. (1864-65).

Records of the U.S. Army Continental Commands, 1821-1920 (Department of the Missouri, District of South West Missouri, Record Group 393).

Index

M

McAllister, John C.: 105
McCall, John ("Jack"): shoots Wild Bill
  Hickok, 174; capture, 174; Deadwood trial
  and acquittal, 175; rearrest and trial at
  Yankton, 175; hanged, 175; alleged
  photograph of, 200; early life, 201
McCanles, David C.: 13; at Rock Creek, Nebr.
  Terr., 13-14, 39ff.; early life, 40
McCanles, Mrs. Mary: 40
McCanles, William Monroe: 14-15
McConnell, Andrew: 127
McCormick, Mrs. Jean Hickok: 186
McCoy's Addition: 107
McCoy, Joseph G.: establishes cattle shipping
  point at Abilene, 105, 124; hires Wild Bill
  Hickok, 106, 124; extension of cattle trail,
  106, 124, 128; court fight with railway
  company, 124-25; death of, 125
McDonald, James H.: 106; shootout with
  Tom Smith's murderers, 126-27
Maeder, Fred G.: 150
Majilton Photographic Co., Philadelphia, Pa.:
  162
Malden, Ill.: 26
Mann, Carl: 174
Mann, John: 174
Martin, Thomas: 57
Massie, Capt. William R.: 174
Maull & Fox (photographers): 78
Maximilian (emperor of Mexico): 135
Meinhold, Capt. Charles: 141
Meixel (photographer): 73
Meline, Col. James F.: 70
Mendota, Ill.: 153
Mersman, Agnes: *see* Mrs. Agnes Lake
  Thatcher
Metropolitan Billiard Hall: 176
Metropolitan Hotel, Omaha, Nebr.: 171
Middleton, "Doc": *see* James M. Riley
Milner, Moses Embree ("California Joe"):
  173, 174, 196
Missouri Border Ruffians: 12, 27ff., 55
Monticello, Kans.: 21
Moore, Catherine: 134-35
Moore, James: 134-35
Mora (photographer): 74

Moreland, Newton: 142
Morlacchi, Guiseppina (Josephine): 146,
  171
Morrow, Stanley J.: 191
Mosby, Col. John S.: 55
Mount Moriah, S.Dak.: 175, 194
Mulvey (Melvin or Mulrey), Bill: shot by Wild
  Bill Hickok, 103

N

Nelson, John Y.: 170
Neuman, A. (photographer): 66
Newcomb, Tom: 196
New Rumley, Ohio: 74, 76
New York, N.Y.: 143, 162
Niagara Falls, Ontario, Canada: 140
Nichols, Col. George Ward: describes
  McCanles fight, 13; describes Hickok's
  Civil War exploits, 56ff., 62ff.; career of, 66;
  death of, 66
Noble's Photographic Gallery, Leavenworth,
  Kans.: 81
North Hero, Vt.: 19, 20
North Platte, Nebr.: 171
Nuttall and Mann's Saloon No. 10,
  Deadwood, Dak. Terr.: 174

O

Oberlin, Kans.: 25, 144
Oglala Sioux: 141
Omaha, Nebr.: 143, 149, 172
Omohundro, John Burwell ("Texas Jack"):
  engaged to capture buffaloes for grand
  buffalo hunt at Niagara Falls, N.Y., 140; on
  stage with Buffalo Bill Cody, 142ff.;
  marriage, 146; hunter, 171; death of, 146
Osceola, Mo.: 52
Otero, Miguel: 115
Otero and Sellars (Hays City, Kans.,
  merchants): 115
Outwell, England: 23
Overton, E. B.: 142-43, 149
Owen, John: 12
Owen, Mary Jane: 12, 22

W

Wallace, Brig. Gen. William H.: 90
Wand, Phoebe: 41
Warren, Rev. W. F.: 182
Washington, D.C.: 14, 71
Washita, Battle of: 61, 72
Waud, A. R.: 39, 64
Webb, William E.: 111, 112
Webster, A. B.: 110
Weiss, Joseph ("Joe"): 110
Wellman, Horace: 14-15
Wellman, Mrs. Horace: 12
Whistler (Sioux): murdered by white men, 141
White, Barclay A.: 142
Whiteford, John: 103
Whiting, Charles C. (U.S. marshal): 102;
    employs Wild Bill Hickok as a deputy, 71,
    108; suspended from office following
    Pawnee Indian massacre, 102; death of,
    104
Whitney, Chauncey B.: 79
Whitney, R. C.: 73
Wichita, Kans.: 106, 125, 140

"Wild Bill": *see* James Butler Hickok
Wild Bill's Outfit: 141-42
Wild Bill the Indian Slayer (dime novel): 88ff.
Wild Bill's First Trail (dime novel): 88ff.
Williams, Michael ("Mike"): shot by Wild Bill
    Hickok by mistake, 107
Wilson, Hill P. (U.S. comm.): 104, 114, 117
Wilson, William: 71
Wilson's Creek, Battle of: 45, 58
Wilson's Creek, Mo.: 45
Wilstach, Frank Jenners: 41; acquired an
    alleged Wild Bill Hickok pistol, 122
Wilstach, Mrs. Frank J.: presents alleged
    Hickok pistol to the Kansas State Historical
    Society, 122
Wolff, George: 84ff.
Wolff, Mary: 85
Woods, James: 14
Woodson, Daniel: 27, 30
Worrall, Henry: 133

Y

Yankton, D. T.: 175, 191

223

Designed by Edward Shaw and Terry Bernardy,
The West of Wild Bill Hickok was composed by the
University of Oklahoma Press in eleven and ten point Souvenir
and printed offset on seventy pound Glatfelter
Offset with presswork and binding by
Halliday Lithography Corporation